World Citizen

Allen Ginsberg as Traveller

by David S. Wills

published by Beatdom Books

Published by Beatdom Books

View the publisher's website:
www.books.beatdom.com

Printed in the United Kingdom
First Print Edition
ISBN 978-0-9934099-6-7

Contents

Also by the Author

About the Beat Generation
Scientologist! William S. Burroughs and the
'Weird Cult' (2013)

Other Works
The Dog Farm (2010)
6 Stories (2014)
Crossing India the Hard Way (2018)
Grammar for IELTS Writing (2018)

Introduction

It's early 2019 and I'm in Florence, Italy, thinking that this book may need an introduction. I'm not exactly sure what needs to be said, as I doubt this will be the first book anyone reads about Allen Ginsberg, so I'll cut past the "Allen Ginsberg was one of the core members of the Beat Generation..." shtick. Yet there are a few things that should and could be said to introduce the book, to prepare the reader.

World Citizen began about five years ago. My first book, *Scientologist! William S. Burroughs and the 'Weird Cult'*, had come out in 2013 and I was looking for a new subject. The Burroughs book had sort of unfolded naturally for me after writing a brief article on it some years earlier, but *Book #2* wasn't exactly forthcoming.

The idea for this book came to me while I was travelling, of course. As a university lecturer, I travel often due to my extensive holidays in the summer and winter months, and I have visited more than forty countries. I toyed with the idea of writing a travel book, but soon realised that I'm not a particularly interesting subject for a book. If only there was a well-travelled Beat writer...

Jack Kerouac is of course the man who wrote the most famous travel book of the twentieth century and sent countless young folks around the world on their own journeys, but he didn't actually do that well out on the road, and preferred being back at home. William S. Burroughs, on the other hand, spent a huge chunk of his life living as an expatriate in Mexico City, Tangier, Paris, and London, but these places were all home to him. He wasn't exactly footloose. And besides, I'd just written a book about him...

When I looked at Allen Ginsberg, it all fell into place. He travelled far and wide, and seemed happier on the road than at home. I tried figuring out how many countries he'd actually visited and couldn't. It took several years to gather the research, and I finally came to the number sixty-six. Sixty-six countries! It is an impressive tally for a man who didn't leave home until... Hold on, I'll let you read ahead and find that out in the book.

This book is intended as a biography of Allen Ginsberg through the prism of travel. This was something I had noted as absent from the already rather extensive library of books about his life and work. As you will see in this book, I have quoted other Ginsberg biographers on the subject of his travels, but there has heretofore been no book explicitly about his travels, nor the impact they had upon his poetry.

If this book were to have a thesis (and it doesn't; it is simply a biography with a slightly odd focus), it would be that travel was very important to Allen. It was travel that helped him find his poetic voice, travel that gave him the inspiration and location for his greatest poems, and travel that shaped his personality and personal image, ultimately creating the public identity of Allen Ginsberg. I have divided the book into four parts, corresponding to the major journeys and periods in his life, beginning with his first forays into the wider world, then looking at his major trips to Europe, South America, and Asia.

I suspect that most readers familiar with Allen Ginsberg's life will find little in this book that is ground-breaking, but I hope that it helps position his life and work in a *slightly* new light. I have been reading and writing about Allen for years, but it was only through the work I did on this book that I came to realise how important travel was to him and his poetry.

Moreover, as an avid traveller (and tourist, if one is to make such distinctions), I was also impressed by his ability to survive in utterly alien environments for long periods of time. Long before Tripadvisor and Google Maps, Ginsberg was able to head off into the unknown with virtually empty pockets, get by on his wits, make money, make friends, and, most importantly, learn about the world. Able to identify with people and make himself at home almost anywhere, Allen Ginsberg was very much a World Citizen.

*

As you may have noticed from the title and my rambling introduction, this book is written in British English. Yes, "traveller" and "travelling" can have two *l*s. What a colourful realisation. Ginsberg himself used both British and American spelling in his writings, depending on his mood and his reading at that particular time, and I have of course kept his spelling when quoting him.

Throughout the book, I have quoted Ginsberg extensively in order to bring his voice into the story, as after all, it is *his* story. I have left his words largely unchanged in order to keep his voice as authentic as possible, so rather than editing "I" to "[he]" and so on, I have simply kept his original text, whether from a poem, letter, journal entry, or interview.

Rather than using footnotes, I have referenced each of the quotes in the book and collected them as endnotes. Again, I chose to do this in order to create a greater sense of immediacy and avoid distractions. These can be found at the end of the text. In the choice between making citations easier to look up and making the book more readable, I elected for the latter.

Finally, this book includes two appendices, which hopefully the reader will find of some additional value. Again, rather than interrupt the flow of the narrative with marginally extraneous information, I have gathered at the back of the book a complete list of Ginsberg's travels, alongside dates, as well as an essay on a mysterious Chinese poem that seemed to have been of some importance to Allen. I have included a translation of the poem, which I think will help readers to better appreciate Ginsberg's own Chinese-inspired poetry.

David S. Wills
January, 2019

Part One:
Learning to Travel
1926-1951

"Shall you voyage? You must alter in your soul.
You must grow beyond your world..."

Childhood

There was little to suggest that the young Allen Ginsberg would grow up to become a great world traveller. One might have looked at his parents and guessed that he, too, would become an outspoken, politically-engaged poet ... but there wasn't much to indicate that he would set out and explore the globe, visiting more than sixty countries, sometimes travelling for years at a time, while relying upon his wits for survival.

Although his mother was born in Russia and his father's family came from what is now Ukraine, Naomi and Louis Ginsberg settled in New York and then later New Jersey, moving very little beyond that. Throughout Allen's childhood, the family moved frequently from home to home and young Allen was constantly uprooted and moved into different schools. Yet all of this took place within a very small area, geographically speaking.

During holidays, the extended Ginsberg clan would take to the beach at Belmar, New Jersey. Occasionally, they would go somewhere else, but they always stayed within New York or New Jersey. Naomi, who didn't get along with her in-laws, insisted one year that they go instead to Woodstock to spend their holiday at an artists' retreat, and twice they visited a Communist Party camp, also in upstate New York. Later, they would visit Arverne, in Queens, near the 1939-40 World's Fair, which the family attended in June, 1940. Despite the dawn of the Second World War, the governments of sixty countries participated in the event, putting on an unprecedented display of culture from across the globe, which surely intrigued young Allen.

All of this movement took place within only two states, and by the time Allen had graduated from high school in 1943, he hadn't travelled much more than one hundred miles from his place of birth. Although American society was taking to the roads and rails with vigour in the first half of the twentieth century, and half of American households now owned a car, not everyone could afford to travel. The Ginsbergs didn't own a car, and relied mostly on buses for transportation.

Louis Ginsberg earned a modest salary as a teacher, and during the Great Depression—which lasted most of Allen's childhood—teachers' salaries were reduced.[1] To make matters worse, Louis had to go into debt to pay for treatment for his wife, who was suffering from severe mental illness and had to be institutionalised. The idea of owning a car, or travelling more than a few hours for vacation, was simply out of the question.

Yet this lack of physical movement never hindered Allen's engagement with the wider world on a mental level. From an early age he avoided the trap of merely thinking of the world in terms of his own existence, and he participated in family discussions on important issues. The Ginsberg household had been divided along political lines since before Allen was born, and throughout his childhood it continued to be a place where politics was openly discussed over the dinner table. When his mother sided with the Communist stance on war, Allen was able to point to Russia and Finland on a world map and demonstrate the vast difference in size between the two countries. Clearly a

4

lack of mobility hadn't hindered his interest in global geography.

Most likely due to his parents' influence, Allen read voraciously on world issues, becoming highly informed and very opinionated. Between 1938 and 1940 he made extensive cuttings from newspapers and summarized headlines in his journal, showing concern not just with the most obvious conflicts, but an awareness of issues in every corner of the globe. His political beliefs varied from year to year, but generally he was opposed to war. He was also opposed to isolationism, believing that the millions of deaths occurring around the world might need to be stopped through U.S. military intervention. He felt strongly that the world needed the League of Nations, sincerely believed in democracy, and argued that there should be a "free humanity."[2] His earliest writings—journal entries, letters—show a mind absolutely engaged with events in China, Europe, and Latin America. Years later, he claimed that in his adolescence he had "dreamed of being a senator or representative or an ambassador."[3]

Beyond politics, Allen was beginning to excel in literature, remarking at age fifteen: "I'll be a genius of some kind or other, probably in literature. I really believe it."[4] Although his literary tastes wouldn't undergo an accelerated development until he was in university, as a child he was influenced by his poet father and read widely. However, during these formative years his greatest interest was watching movies. His first journals are filled with records of movies he watched and the cinemas he visited. Sometimes he would sit and watch a movie over and over. "They afford me great pleasure and are about the only relief from boredom which seems to hang around me like a shadow," he explained, although one could also assume they were an escape from the trauma of witnessing his mother's tragic deterioration.[5] In any case, these books and movies served up yet another window on the world for a boy who was bursting with curiosity, but lacking the power to get out and see it for himself.

College

In 1942, after the United States had entered the Second World War, Allen's older brother, Eugene, joined the Air Force and was sent off to the United Kingdom. Back home, Allen lamented the dropping of the draft age from twenty to eighteen. He was now sixteen years old, and he had no desire to go off and fight, regardless of any political conviction about defending the free world.

Ginsberg was accepted into Columbia University on 14th May, 1943, and after graduating from East Side High School at the end of June, he immediately enrolled in summer term classes and began his university career. In high school he had excelled in English and foreign languages, and at university he would continue to pursue these areas of study, taking English and French classes. In class, he studied copious classic works under Lionel Trilling, Mark Van Doren, and Raymond Weaver, but most importantly, he learned of new writers through his friends—Lucian Carr, William

S. Burroughs, and Jack Kerouac. Carr's bookshelf was filled with works in French, and Burroughs' books were almost entirely unheard of to Ginsberg—Kafka, Cocteau, Céline, and Baudelaire. Increasingly, Ginsberg turned away from politics and towards his newfound interest in literature, becoming particularly taken by the young French poet, Arthur Rimbaud, and others whom his new friends recommended.

As is evident from any biography of Allen Ginsberg, his Columbia years were among the most important in his life, and, indeed, this period became a turning point in twentieth century American literature, as it marked the birth of what later became known as the Beat Generation. Ginsberg's friendship with Carr, Burroughs, and Kerouac, among others, has been extensively documented. What drew him to these men was not just a shared interest in literature, or even a sexual attraction. Ginsberg looked up to each of them and learned from his older and wiser companions. They were all worldly compared to naïve young Allen. They had more life experience than he had—except, perhaps, concerning mental illness—and had all travelled more than him. Kerouac had already shipped out with the Merchant Marine on a dangerous wartime run to Greenland, while the much older Burroughs had lived and studied in Europe. Ginsberg was drawn to Burroughs for his experience of "the glorious artistic time of the Weimar Rep[ublic] . . . true, free, a Bohemian culture . . ."[6] as well as his sharp wit and extensive knowledge. "Burroughs educated me more than Columbia," he recalled, decades later.[7]

In his other friends, Ginsberg looked for similar qualities. One of his early friends at Columbia was a man named John Kingsland, whom Ginsberg considered "worldly-wise," and another was a "Jap" who introduced him to Japanese cuisine—despite the on-going war between their respective nations.[8] Allen, who took a scientific eye to all his early experiences, was eager to compare it with "the Chinese delicacies" he'd previously encountered.[9] As a boy, his favourite foods came from Eastern Europe, and although these would remain his favourites throughout his life, he was always curious to try new things.

Preparing for the Voyage

Though the following years were ones of intense personal discovery for Ginsberg, he still remained in New York, occasionally returning to New Jersey. His mind was expanding with new thoughts and ideas and influences, but physically he had no opportunities to get out and explore the world. In August, 1944, he dreamed of hitchhiking through France or England with Carr and another friend, Arthur Lazarus, and that same day he wrote a "Romanticized Version of a Tragedy" in which he imagines or recalls sitting in the West End bar that his social group often frequented. In his account, David Kammerer and Lucian Carr were planning to ship out, while another friend, Walter Adams, was planning a motorcycle trip. One gets a sense of the alienation Allen felt watching his friends go off and see the world—

even if it was just a trip to Vermont. When asked if he, too, would like to join his friends, who are "traveling souls," he replies that to do so would be "foolishly valorous, and therefore indiscreet."[10] Also evident is a slight fear of travel, which is apparent in his early attempts at poetry, beginning around this time.

The day after Ginsberg wrote these two journal entries, Lucian Carr killed David Kammerer, in what became a pivotal moment in Beat history. Ginsberg felt a sense of isolation as his group of friends split and people vanished in the wake of the tragedy. "The libertine circle is destroyed," he noted. It seemed to him that everyone was going off somewhere else, and that he was the only person stuck in the same place: "only I will remain faithful to the past."[11]

The event can be said to have spurred the group of young libertines into metamorphosing from pretentious, postulating students into creative artists, although that is perhaps an oversimplification. In any case, when Carr went to serve time for the incident, which was judged to be an act of self-defence, Ginsberg's primary influences became Burroughs and Kerouac. Kerouac considered himself a serious writer and, although he professed little interest in writing at the time, Burroughs' recommended reading was to cast an immense influence over Ginsberg's burgeoning literary ambitions. Until this point, Allen's father and brother were the family poets, but in 1944, Ginsberg began to identify as a poet and wrote his first serious poems. One, called "The Last Voyage," which he finished in 1945, is clearly modelled upon Rimbaud's

"Le Bateau Ivre" and Baudelaire's "Le Voyage." It begins:

> Others have voyaged far, have sailed
> On waves that wash beyond the world[12]

He later dismissed the poem as an "immense piece of juvenilia"[13] which was highly imitative of his father's poetry, and indeed it is only really of interest as evidence of how derivative his earliest work was, particularly in comparison to the inventive poet he later became. However, it also suggests that he considered voyages as exciting and romantic, yet too perilous for him to seriously consider. One line in his poem asks, "Oh, is my journeying my doom?"[14] The reader then must wonder whether his imagined voyager is simply a character based upon Rimbaud, the young poet who travelled to far-flung corners of the globe, Baudelaire's mysterious journeyman, or one of his own better-travelled friends from Columbia. The poem may simply be an imitation, or it may well reflect his envy, or fear, concerning travel. Certainly, his mindset at the time suggests a mix of all three.

In Rimbaud's poem, the sixteen-year-old poet imagines a boat drifting at sea, taking on water (hence, "drunken") and finally sinking into the ocean. Similarly, but more cryptically, Baudelaire's poem details a voyage ending in death, which is itself but a new journey. Ginsberg's homage doesn't appear to end so bleakly, with his voyage at sea simply returning him to where he began, having barely skirted disaster:

Thus I finish my last journey.
This, my ship, has found its berth,
And on anchoring, has turned me
Back to the harbor of the earth.[15]

This poem is also noteworthy as it featured in a
planned novel. In late 1944, Ginsberg was attempting—
as did Kerouac and Burroughs—to write a book based
upon the Carr-Kammerer incident. In his plans for
the novel, the final chapter and epilogue have Kerouac
going off to sea and Burroughs moving to Persia,
while Ginsberg remains in New York, writing "The
Last Voyage." Yet again, he is romanticizing travel,
but seems resigned to his fate of never actually going
anywhere. He is doomed to watch his friends go off on
perilous, heroic journeys while he simply stays at home
and writes about how dangerous it would be to see the
world.

At the beginning of the novel, though Kerouac's
character laments having to go off to sea, which he's
tired of, Ginsberg's character is jealous:

We sat around in front of the dock talking
about his trip. He thought that he was
going to France. I hoped so and wished I
could go.[16]

Though he had made no obvious declarations of
desire to travel, or even attempted to do so, it is easy to
believe that he wished he could go to France. Though
fearful and timid, he was filled with a deep curiosity

about the world that is evident in his words and actions from childhood onwards. In 1945, the year he would finally break free from the confines of his New York-New Jersey borders, he wrote in his journal: "Curiosity is the only thing that keeps me from suicide."[17] His interest in art and culture and people and politics made it clear that he was cut out for travel, and that his lack of movement prior to 1945 was just a matter of circumstance—it would have been difficult, if not destructive, for him to have done anything different. Perhaps not "foolishly valorous," but certainly not the most sensible choice. Still, as a curious young man, it was just a matter of time before he made his foray into the wider world. As his biographer, Michael Schumacher, observed in an annotation to the collection of letters between Allen and Louis Ginsberg, "Allen's immense curiosity made him a natural traveler."[18]

Shipping Out

In March, 1945, Ginsberg was suspended from Columbia University for writing obscenities on his dorm room window, and having had Kerouac—an unwanted person on campus—stay the night in his room. He soon moved in with Joan Adams, John Kingsland, and Hal Chase, and continued his studies of life and literature under William Burroughs, who replaced his professors, in the various bars of Eighth Avenue, which became his new school.

However, within a few months the inevitable had

occurred and Ginsberg was looking beyond New York and out at the wider world. As so many of his friends had done, he signed up for the Merchant Marine, and on 30th July he moved to Sheepshead Bay to learn the skills needed to work at sea. He wrote Kerouac, who was in France at the time, to say it was *"Incipit vita nuova!"* — the beginning of a new life.[19] It was, however, not to be a permanent move, and he remarked that he fully intended to return to Columbia to finish his academic education. But his expectations of life in the Merchant Marine were evidently high, as he speculated that his eventual return to Columbia might just be "only a pilgrimage of acceptance of former time."[20] Indeed, although he clearly viewed life at sea as somewhat romantic and exciting, ultimately it was a good way to make money, and if he was ever to return to Columbia, he would need cash to continue his studies.

At the U.S. Maritime Service Training Station at Sheepshead Bay, Allen spent more than three months earning his Seaman's Union card. He gained important real-life experience here, working hard at first, scrubbing floors, cleaning the latrines, and washing dishes, but soon realised that the important thing was simply to do the hours and make it seem like he had worked hard. He didn't take well to the rigid discipline and complained that "There is a great deal of stupidity in the management" which was run by "fat buttocked Marine sergeants with loud voices."[21] However, he was able to view it as a temporary situation and a useful life experience. He learned how to be "a regular fellow" and "one of the boys" by swearing, adopting a new accent, and making racist remarks. To counterbalance the Hart Crane, Arthur Rimbaud, and yoga books that he had brought, he purchased a copy of *Batman*—"my passport to this corner of reality."[22] He had no desire to be labelled as an intellectual there. As with his studies of the various types of people in the bars of New York, he seemed proud of his sociological analyses as well as his ability to fit in.

Ginsberg came to enjoy the experience, particularly after he discovered the nearby Manhattan Beach, where he spent his weekends swimming and lounging around. However, it was no surprise that the discipline of military life was difficult for him to cope with for very long, and by September he had been admitted to the Training Center Hospital with pneumonia. As he recuperated in the comparatively comfortable sick bay, he continued his extensive reading and wrote long letters, including a passionate defence of his hero, Rimbaud, to his former professor and friend, Lionel Trilling. Burroughs enrolled at Sheepshead Bay while Ginsberg was in the infirmary, but he was there only two days and left without seeing his friend.

In November, after three and a half months' training, Ginsberg received his Seaman's Union card and had saved $103.79. During his stay at Sheepshead Bay, the United States had dropped atomic bombs on Hiroshima and Nagasaki, ending the war and ensuring a relative degree of safety in any future work at sea. Ginsberg was now qualified to work on commercial freighters, and on the day he graduated, 17th November, he immediately shipped out as a messman, headed for Norfolk, Virginia on a slow transport vessel called *Crossing Hitch*. Although the posting lasted only a week, it was the furthest he had ever ventured from home.

After Norfolk, an option arose to sail to Venezuela, but this opportunity never came to pass, and on 27th December, he shipped out instead on the *S.S. Groveton*, a barge headed for New Orleans. In New Orleans, he smoked marijuana with Puerto Rican sailors in a brothel, and on the trip there he was afforded time to read and write. On the barge, he completed "Ode to Decadence," which "has absorbed most of my literary energy" for the previous three months.[23] This is an important poem in that it was the first in which Ginsberg used a new language he'd uncovered while studying the denizens of Times Square and the sailors in the Merchant Marine. He sent the poem to Trilling, calling attention to the "jive talk" that it featured. Much of the poem is reminiscent of Rimbaud, whom Ginsberg continued to read while sailing, but the section which features the aforementioned "jive talk" marks a significant departure and is, perhaps, the first example of Ginsberg finding his own voice, or at least borrowing a voice not from another writer, but from his friends and from people in the "Underworld." It is the first of Ginsberg's poems that one could look back through and call "Ginsbergian." It is also, interestingly, perhaps the earliest written evidence of the word "Beat" as applied to his generation:

>   . . .you
> Are left hung up and beat, a broken square,
> Nauseous with hallucination, dumb[24]

The trip was full of highs and lows for the fledgling sailor. Three days after leaving New York, he became seasick and "experienced what must have been at least one of the most agonizing depressions known to man."[25] He felt the journey was pointless as the ship was empty and no one on board yet knew they were heading to New Orleans. Allen was nineteen years old and heading out on the longest voyage of his life, and he was experiencing what any young man or woman would feel in a similar situation—a crushing sense of homesickness. Still, after a few weeks he was floating on the Gulf of Mexico, "in Hart Crane seas," as he remarked, under blue skies and surrounded by staggering beauty. "Really," he wrote Trilling, "I do enjoy sailing in these tropical waters, in watching the stars, in inventing fabulous romances on the prow of the ship as she bounces forward."[26] Another point of interest here is that he appears to have assembled lines from previous letters and journal entries into a new poem, which he sent Trilling. This poetic technique is something he would use frequently much later in life.

In mentioning that he was "in Hart Crane" seas, Allen is admitting another of his literary travel influences. Crane was another American poet inspired by Rimbaud and Whitman, and was homosexual like Allen. He had travelled France and Mexico before committing suicide by jumping from a ship into the Gulf of Mexico. Ginsberg admired Crane for bridging a gap between old and new styles of poetry, and carrying a Whitmanic spirit into the twentieth century for others, like the Beat poets, to continue. One of Crane's poems contains a nod to Whitman: "The seas all crossed, weathered the Capes, the voyage done." Ginsberg considered this "one of the prettiest things ever written about Whitman by a later American follower."[27] Allen also enjoyed Crane's "Voyages," which was set on the Caribbean, and is probably what Allen referred to above by "Hart Crane seas." A few decades later Ginsberg acknowledged taking some images from this poem to use in "Howl."[28] One can see Crane's influence in other contemporary Ginsberg poems, too.

In June, 1946, he shipped out once again on the *S.S. Jagger Seam*, working for the oddly named Mystic Steamship Company ("which is pleasing, though it doesn't make the coal dust any less filthy"), delivering coal up and down the east coast over a two-month period.[29] Though he did not venture so far on this trip, and was even permitted to return home when dropping anchor near New Jersey, he was nevertheless afflicted with homesickness, and quoted Ezra Pound several times in his journal: "I am homesick after my own kind."[30] Once again, he was given plenty of time to read and write, and on this journey he produced what he considered his best poem yet, "Death in Violence," which he also referred to as "Death of the Voyager." This is important, as throughout his life, and for various reasons, travel would allow him the opportunity to make significant poetic breakthroughs. However, with characteristic melodrama, he announced that it would likely be his final poem, as he was not entirely satisfied with it.

"Death in Violence" marks another milestone in the development of Ginsberg's poetry away from classical verse. It is a prose poem that moves closer to his own voice, although it is nonetheless heavily influenced by his reading at the time—namely, W.H. Auden and Crane. In fact, it references many authors, most of whom were introduced to Ginsberg by Burroughs, to whom the poem was dedicated. Yet it also cites people Ginsberg knew, like Herbert Huncke, who also appeared in "Ode to Decadence." The poem begins, fascinatingly, with a reference to those whom he would later dub his "best minds":

> O heroes, hipsters, humanists, Prometheans!
> arrange your lives as best you can before the
> voyage—[31]

The narrative is aimed, seemingly, as advice to those mentioned above. Ginsberg uses his own experiences and ideas cribbed from his reading list to address the dangers of nameless voyages. As he wrote this poem, he was floating on a ship towards somewhere he didn't know, leaving behind everyone he knew and loved, and that sense of hopelessness and fear comes through the lines of this long poem. It is filled with confessionalism, something that would mark most of his later poetry. This is especially true in the lines that directly refer to voyages:

The tears you'll shed before your early eyes fall
     out,
gouged by the stretching shadows of the cities
     and
the seas you'll cross, the tears as uncontrollable
     as sleep
these tears shall have been shed sufficient to
     their cause.

I pity your first aimless journey, your virgin
     hatred
of yourself, and your confused inconsistency
to origins and endings in the unaccustomed
wilderness within, without . . . the moist disgust[32]

Although given as advice, it is full of questions and uncertainty. It seems he is writing as much for himself as anyone else. He asks,

Shall you voyage? You must alter in your soul.
You must grow beyond your world, your city of
millennial foundations sinking in the earth.[33]

The last line in the above quote is annotated in a version of the poem later sent to Neal Cassady as a reference to Oswald Spengler, whose book, *The Decline of the West*, was of major interest to the three core members of the Beat Generation. If the poem is, indeed, asking questions of himself, then clearly he is looking beyond this short money-making trip to New Orleans to further voyages into the wider world in search of much more. And while he may be doing this to explore the world or himself, he is also considering an idea that intrigued both Kerouac and Burroughs—that the western, or at least American, civilisation is on the decline, perhaps even in its death throes.

On the Road for Neal Cassady

During the summer of 1946, Ginsberg applied to be readmitted to Columbia and, after securing the positive recommendation of a psychiatrist, he was allowed to attend the autumn semester, beginning 20th September. In the past, he had studied various languages with some success, and this term he elected to study Arabic, though he wrote of planning to drop it in favour of a course on Chinese history. From Burroughs, he was learning about Egyptian, Chinese, and Mayan writing systems, and in his personal reading he was attempting to learn some Chinese characters. Ginsberg had an interest in all things Chinese—especially politics, food, and culture—throughout most of his life.

Late in the year, Neal Cassady arrived in New York City and he and Ginsberg met for the first time, although they didn't properly get to know each other until January. Naturally, Allen fell in love with Neal, as was the recurring pattern throughout his life with every sensitive, charismatic, handsome man he met. They began a sexual relationship that was fraught with troubles—namely, Cassady's avowed heterosexuality—and Ginsberg fell into a state of depression. He became almost suicidal, looked into psychoanalysis, and had dreams of fleeing to Europe. On 7th March, Cassady returned to Denver and, such were Ginsberg's feelings, he decided to make the trip to Denver at the end of the Columbia school year.

After a successful spring semester, Allen took off for Denver via Texas in early June, where he planned to drop-in on the Burroughses at their farm in New Waverly, fifty miles north of Houston. The trip was, perhaps ominously, paid for by prize money ("almost $150") he had unexpectedly won for his poem, "Death in Violence."[34] In their letters, Ginsberg and Cassady talked about meeting in Texas and returning to Denver together, but when Allen arrived, there was a letter waiting for him from Neal, explaining that he no longer intended to come to Texas, but encouraging Allen to make the journey west himself—and to bring marijuana from the farm.[35] Neal suggested that they might make the trip back to Texas in August together, and thence onwards to New York. He didn't hide the fact that he had met another woman, Carolyn Robinson, yet evidently this was something Ginsberg failed to see as an obstacle in their relationship.

The trip to Texas was the longest that Allen had made by road, and the farm must have seemed exotic to the boy from the big city. The weather was intensely hot and humid, and there were animals Ginsberg had never seen before: tics, chiggers, scorpions, and armadillos. He was particularly fascinated by the armadillos and their "kind of stupid and pure mechanism of conduct."[36] Burroughs, who knew the beasts well, was able to capture one and bring it indoors for Allen to examine. Burroughs' "farm," however, was more of a cabin in the woods, with a few other broken-down buildings dotted around, far from any of his neighbours, where he grew marijuana. The soil wasn't good enough to grow much else. He had previously attempted to be a "gentleman farmer" with his friend, Kells Elvins, but he had no real farming knowledge, and the experiment was a colossal failure. As they had been in New York City, the tenants of the New Waverly farm, including the heavily pregnant Joan, were heavy users of various substances. Even notorious addict Huncke was concerned about Joan's Benzedrine use. Allen sometimes worked in the fields, but mostly sat on the porch, talking and listening to music. Still, the experience seemed to be a positive one, as he wrote Lionel Trilling a month later:

> I hadn't ever before been on a farm and this was a wonderful introduction to one—bayou, Spanish moss, scorpions, good company, isolation, a little work when I felt like it, a hand-wound Victrola with lots of be-bop records, woods to explore, trees to climb, a Jeep to learn to drive, weekend trips to Houston, etc.[37]

In July, Ginsberg took a Greyhound bus to Denver, where he was met at the terminal by Cassady and taken to a nearby hotel. It soon became clear to Ginsberg that the trip was a mistake, as Cassady was involved with Carolyn. Neal's letters had told Allen that this was the case, and that he wasn't interested in homosexual sex, but Allen had for some reason persisted, ensuring the visit would be painful. Soon he had run out of money and was sleeping in the same room as the couple, torn apart by jealousy as he listened to them having sex in the night. Although Carolyn failed to understand the reason for Allen's unhappiness, the relationship between them was tense.

As the summer advanced, Ginsberg fell into a deep depression. Cassady was sleeping with numerous women, but not with Allen. They had long conversations in the middle of the night at the beginning of summer, but, as time went by, Cassady would fail to show up at the small apartment Ginsberg found near Neal and Carolyn's hotel. Still, as with other voyages, this trip to Denver yielded important advancements in his poetry. On 23rd August, his final day in Denver, it occurred to him that in his journal he had written much about himself and Neal, but nothing about Denver as a place. He began "sketching" what he saw, using a method recommended by Kerouac. Five years later, using a technique suggested by William Carlos Williams, he rearranged his journal notes into a poem called "The Bricklayer's Lunch Hour." It is one of his finest early poems, and a marked departure from previous efforts, including the dense and opaque effort that had also resulted from his time in Colorado, "Denver Doldrums."

The journey he'd taken to Denver, via New Waverly, was also important in his development as a traveller. Prior to this, he'd only ever travelled through his work on ships, but now he was learning how to survive on his own on the road. The skills he developed here would be honed in the coming years, eventually making him into a master traveller, capable of not only surviving, but truly making the most out of his journeys around the world. He had come to Denver with the expectation that Neal would provide him with a job, a place to stay, and perhaps even some financial help—not to mention the emotional support that he craved. However, none of this materialised, and Allen was forced to look after himself in this strange new city, two thousand miles from home. He wrote a friend, "Now I am in Denver, broke, hungry, unemployed, depressed."[38]

Fortunately, he soon made friends with two nurses that Cassady knew, and they gave him food, shelter, and "cigarette money."[39] Allen's ability to meet new people and make friends easily would help him immensely in future travels. Then he found a job as a night porter for the May Company, and spent his paycheque on a basement apartment. From the department store where he worked, he stole some clothes to improve his appearance, among other items. He also utilised the skills he'd learned at Sheepshead Bay to avoid actually doing much work, and instead listened to music for most of his shift. In the month and a half he spent in Denver, though he was filled with self-loathing, and remained hopelessly attached to Neal, he nonetheless matured and developed skills that would serve him well in the future.

Leaving America

In late July, Allen asked Neal to accompany him to Texas. He'd planned this much earlier, even asking Huncke to build them a bed in anticipation of the wild sex Allen hoped would take place. However, in Denver it had been increasingly obvious that Allen's affections were misplaced and that any long-term sexual or romantic relationship between the two men was pure fantasy on Allen's part. Nevertheless, Cassady agreed, and several weeks later they took off for New Waverly together.

They hitch-hiked from Denver—leaving at 2 am one morning, travelling down through Oklahoma and Texas—to New Waverly, leaving behind the mighty Rocky Mountains, traversing the endless plains, and entering bayou country. Their journey took two days. In a story often told through Ginsberg's writings, in the middle of Oklahoma, at an empty intersection as night began to fall, he and Cassady knelt and pledged their souls to one another in a "vow to stick with each other and be spiritual lovers, if not physical."[40] It was key moment in Ginsberg's life, although he realised years later that it meant almost nothing to Cassady.

When they arrived, they found life on the farm in even more disarray than usual, with Burroughs short on money, and Joan and Huncke scraping by with a diminished supply of amphetamines. As could be expected, the trip was unsatisfactory for both Ginsberg and Cassady. It began with Huncke's failure to produce a bed on time for the honeymooning couple—which is how Allen viewed them—and continued as Ginsberg finally came to understand that the relationship was doomed. They had sex from time to time, using the bedroom Huncke kindly gave up for them, but there was no love in the sense that Allen wanted. He began to contemplate the troubles that would develop further down the road as they returned to New York together, and determined that the situation was simply hopeless.

Within a week of arriving on the farm, Ginsberg had made up his mind to leave. There was no hope of any future with Cassady, something that had been obvious to everyone but Ginsberg for a long time. He claimed to have enjoyed "the serenity of the bayou," but by 3rd September he was already in Houston, at the Union Hall, and had accepted a job as a messman on a ship to Marseille, France, going via Gibraltar. He wrote his father to say he was "so disgusted with personal & financial & aesthetic problems that shipping out seemed the only way out."[41] Initially, he had wanted to find a ship headed for New York so that he could arrive back in time for the new semester with a pocketful of much-needed cash, but by 3rd September he had already made up his mind that he was going to miss the semester: "I've decided not to enter till January for obvious reasons. Financial & emotional are predominant."[42] As Cassady later wrote to Kerouac, "He shipped out partially for money. The other reason is me."[43] From Ginsberg's journals, it seems likely that he dreaded being in New York at the same time as Cassady.

The freighter to Marseille wasn't scheduled to leave until the sixth, so he returned to the farm for a few days.

Then, on the fifth, Ginsberg, Cassady, and Huncke drove together to Houston. Huncke was looking for drugs, while Cassady had promised Allen one last night of sex. Allen even borrowed money from Burroughs to pay for the room. However, Cassady managed to enrage both Ginsberg and Huncke by picking up a young, possibly mentally-handicapped girl to sleep with. Cassady's actions were so abhorrent that Huncke felt embarrassed by association, and Allen remonstrated with him so much the following morning that he missed his departure, landing him in hot water with the Maritime Union. They returned to the farm, where Burroughs was furious that they'd forgotten to buy ice and thus ruined all his frozen food. The next day, Cassady drove Ginsberg back to Houston, where he spent a few days "stealing Pepsi-Cola bottles to cash in and buy candy bars for hunger."[44]

Although Ginsberg now knew he was a homosexual and had admitted as much to many of his friends, he had not yet told his father, and so Louis was confused and worried to hear from his son as Allen seemed to cavort aimlessly around the West. The little boy who'd grown up close to home and been engrossed in his studies was now under the influence of miscreants and threatening to throw his whole life away, or so it appeared. His letters from the West had been unbalanced and clearly upset Louis. Allen sought to allay his father's fears in a letter written from on board his next ship, on 12th September, the day it left port:

If you need reassurance, I have (& always had) every intention of getting my degree. My motives in shipping out are spiritual, to be sure (I'm tired of everybody) but are predominantly practical, and I embark mostly for financial reasons. I will come back with a few hundred dollars, I expect (and some souvenirs). I am flat broke otherwise, and I don't want to have to squeeze thru another term borrowing money, & trying to live on $15 a week. Of course I could go back & work part time, but I also want psychoanalysis and that will take a lot more money, & the only thing for me to do, Lou, is to do what I'm doing. Aside from that, it will be healthful & will be a pleasant experience. I've already gained weight & my physique, curiously enough, is already improved; further, I feel finer than I have in a long time, and wait departure with much amiable anticipation, etc. etc.[45]

Clearly, the purpose of this letter was to make his worried father feel better, and the last lines quoted above are probably not entirely true. His motivation for shipping out was more to do with the "spiritual" reasons mentioned first, as well as financial ones. His time at sea earned him a lot of money, and he certainly did intend to undergo psychoanalysis. In March he had written to Wilhelm Reich (of whose work Burroughs was an advocate) for advice, and he'd mentioned analysis in his previous 3rd September letter to Louis, stressing then that it was probably the most important factor in his decision to ship out. However, if he was trying to make his father feel better, he probably failed when he asked Louis to inform his school that he would not be attending the fall semester. Allen certainly intended to return in the spring and graduate the following June, but he had foolishly neglected to inform Columbia that he would not be attending the semester that commenced only a week after he left the U.S.

Amazingly, despite all the negative things that happened to him on his journey that summer, he claimed not to have regretted it. He lamented the suffering he had brought upon himself through "blunders of my own will," but said "the experience has been more salutary than I can describe."[46] Certainly, he had learned a lot about himself, about life, and even made poetic breakthroughs on this seemingly doomed journey.

On 12th September, 1947, he shipped out as a utility man on a collier, the *S.S. John Blair*, for the Ponchelet Marine Corporation. It departed from Freeport, seventy-five miles south of Houston, going through Galveston, passing near Cuba and Haiti—whose mountains Allen watched pass by—and headed for Dakar, capital of the federation of French West Africa, in what is now known as Senegal. Dakar, on the western coast of Africa, had a long colonial history; although, like most European colonial possessions, by 1947 it was nearing the end of its subjugation. Once a major trading port for African slaves, Dakar had a strategic location that ensured its privileged position within the French Empire. The French West African territories were placed under the control of a single governor, who was located in Dakar, and so it had become a seat of power in the region. Indeed, by the early twentieth century, it had become a major city in the empire. As rights were slowly and inconsistently handed out to "French subjects"— i.e. the Africans whose homelands had been annexed by the French—the people born in Dakar were the first to be given the right to vote, and it was from here that the first ever black African elected to the French government was born, Blaise Diagne. A year before Allen's visit, the French Empire had rebranded itself the French Union to give the appearance of equality, and more limited rights were being rolled out; however, more substantial change was on the horizon, with independence just over a decade away.

Though Ginsberg professed to care deeply for a "free humanity" and in equal rights for all men, at times wondering if he should curtail his poetry efforts as a means of devoting himself to an older goal of becoming a labour lawyer and fighting more directly for people's rights, he was nonetheless drawn to somewhat colonial era ideas of Africa. He was "longing for" Africa as a "mysterious" dark land where he could find a native boy to sleep with. He was also keen to find opium and experience life in this exotic land, no doubt excited to follow in the footsteps of his poet hero, Rimbaud— albeit on the opposite side of the giant continent. His rather less literary influences were *Tarzan* and *Bomba*, *the Jungle Boy*—a slightly more racist version of *Tarzan* in comic book and movie form from his youth—which he noted had informed his expectations of Africa.

The 5,000 mile journey to Africa involved twenty days on the way out, ten days in port at Dakar, and twenty days back. As the *S.S. John Blair* approached Dakar, the westernmost point of Africa, Allen was in yet another fit of despair, and contemplating suicide by throwing himself into the sea as Hart Crane had done. As recounted by Bill Morgan in his biography, *I Celebrate Myself*, Ginsberg stood on deck, holding the rail, staring into the dark ocean. He was going to jump into the water—a silent, romantic death—but then the lights of Dakar appeared, and the crew set about preparing for their arrival, forestalling his suicide. He hadn't left a suicide note, he realised, although he had previously drafted several in his journals.[47]

His chief poetic output from the journey to Dakar was a series of poems collected as "Dakar Doldrums." As with the "Denver Doldrums" he'd previously written, these sorrowful poems address his mental state as he pities himself for loving Neal Cassady. Throughout the poem, written in classical language, rather than the "hepcat" voice he had previously developed, he laments his suffering during his "sacramental passage." They also act as a sort of journal, which Ginsberg later called a "psychic diary", for his experiences at sea.[48]

> Twenty days have drifted in the wake
> Of this slow aged ship that coal
> From Texas to Dakar. I, for the sake

Of little but my casualessness of soul
Am carried out of my chill hemisphere
To unfamiliar summer on the earth.
I spend my days to meditate a fear
Each day I give the sea is one of death.[49]

This was another poem about a voyage that would win Ginsberg a poetry prize—the Columbia Boar's Head competition in 1948. Although his own journeys—at sea and on land—were marked by depression, they were artistically fruitful, giving him subject matter for his poetry, time to write, and often allowing him time to develop breakthroughs in form, structure, or voice. Here, Ginsberg subverted the traditional mode by secretly dedicating the poem to Cassady. A reader in 1948 would have assumed the first line: "Most dear, and dearest at this moment, most" was addressed to a woman.

In spite of his self-pity, Ginsberg felt strongly enough about his work to submit "Dakar Doldrums" to the competition, though he had remarked in a letter to Cassady: "I have two hundred beautiful lines from Dakar and I don't care about it except to show you and have you praise me for them."[50]

When they arrived at Dakar—the first time Ginsberg ever set foot on foreign soil—they were surrounded by "dozens of blacks" who dressed in white shorts or trousers and typically went shirtless or wore ragged shirts. Lots of local boys attempted to sell things to the sailors, including women and marijuana. Ginsberg, who had studied French in school, was able to communicate with them, including one of the "natives" who was willing to do all of his work for him, which was mainly kitchen porter duties like scrubbing pots and pans and peeling potatoes.[51] All Allen had to do was light the fire and make sure the "native" was doing his job, while he sat back reading and writing until the evening. For someone ostensibly opposed to colonialism, it was a surprising thing to boast about in his letters. It is nonetheless interesting to observe the development of this skill, which Ginsberg had developed in previous journeys, of avoiding doing too much work so as to maximise his literary efforts.

Despite remarking to Herbert Huncke that Dakar "looks like a perfect second hand copy of Texas," and saying that he felt very much at home there, he also described it in terms that rather set it apart from Texas or, for that matter, anywhere he'd previously visited:

> Lots of adobe huts, grass shacks, modern-
> istic plastic government buildings, nutty
> colonials, beggars etc ... people in fantastic
> costumes dancing around the fire with [a]
> dozen tom-toms.[52]

He seemed to thoroughly enjoy Dakar, in contrast with the depression he'd suffered on board the S.S. *John Blair*. He told Huncke that he was "sent," which means "ecstatic" in hipster talk, and said, "this place is so mad I'm overwhelmed." To his father, he wrote that he was "having a wild time" and echoed his remarks above about it being similar to Texas.[53] He was able to easily acquire marijuana for "a penny a stick" but lamented that "sex is nowhere here" even though he had commissioned someone to find boys for him to sleep with.[54] His terms were that the boys must be fifteen or sixteen years old, desperate for money, and handsome. It was only on his final day in Dakar that Allen's source found him a boy. Alas, the boy in question appears to have been handicapped, and, although desperate, Ginsberg could not bring himself to take advantage of the poor kid, whom he paid off before returning to the ship. Dakar had not been as exciting as he had hoped, and he had failed to find either the opium or uninhibited homosexual intercourse that he wanted, but it is clear from his letters that overall it was a positive experience. Several years later, he would be telling stories "about Dakar witch doctors and New Orleans whorehouses," making himself out to be quite the experienced voyager.[55]

In addition to his long poem, "Dakar Doldrums," another significant piece of work that emerged from the trip to Africa was his short story, "The Monster of Dakar." In fact, it is clear that when comparing the so-called short story to Ginsberg's actual experiences, it was more of a creative memoir than a piece of fiction, and a few years later, in his journal, he contemplated editing it into an actual short story, whereas currently it was "an actual confession."[56] While in his "Dakar Doldrums" poetry, he simply disguised his lover's gender, he labelled his prose as fiction and allowed his narrator to admit his homosexuality. This, too, would be submitted to a literary competition after a few years, though he did not win the first prize, which was a trip to Paris.

In the story, Ginsberg's protagonist is looking back on the year 1947 from the future, remarking that in the middle of that year he was "out on my own in the world for the first time" and briefly reflects upon his failed relationship with Cassady. From there, he recounts his life on the seas, colourfully portraying a diverse crew of misfits, including a handsome Texan who appears like a hybrid of Lucian Carr and Neal Cassady. He says of his expectations for Africa:

> We were headed for Dakar which in my mind I had already equipped with a white stepped Casbah, incense, opium, hashish, Arabian boys, a foreign colony of broken down middle European intellectuals, everybody talking French or Arabic, and the backwoods jungles, with moth-eaten or beautiful Africans, as the case might be. (The map showed a desert and that was fine.) I longed to see Africa, it was my first trip to that great continent, I knew all about it instinctively.
>
> My plan for Africa was an orgy of drugs and native boys: to smoke opium at last, something I had never done, and buy a man and have a totally uninhibited ball for the first time in my life. I had visions of a dark hotel room or a mud hut, nakedness, fire light and a dirt floor.[57]

35

Interestingly, mirroring his work from Denver, Dakar as a physical place warranted little description: "The town itself was nothing. It's just a new port town with no traditions of its own." Instead, Ginsberg describes his own thoughts and desires and activities. He is the titular monster, drawn to prey upon the uneducated, underage, and possibly mentally-handicapped local boys—"That's why I set out from America to begin with," he claims. He also captures the people—the sailors on the ship from Puerto Rico and Texas, as well as the local men and boys in Dakar, including a group of lepers.

Returning to America

Ginsberg arrived back in America about 30th October, sailing into New York. In a letter to Herbert Huncke, he had mentioned that the ship may go further south, to Duala, Cameroon, before sailing for New York, but it is unclear whether or not he did. There is a famous photo of Allen standing on the deck as the ship moved through the harbour, smiling slyly whilst he smokes some marijuana he smuggled back. He may have left the United States in a fit of despair, but the long trip to New York, via Africa, had put him in a better frame of mind, at least temporarily.

Back in New York, he immediately commenced therapy, as he had promised, using the money he earned at sea. On the advice of his therapist, he confessed to his father that he was a homosexual, but he refused to take Doctor Cott's strong suggestion that he give up smoking pot. He was convinced that it wasn't just "for kicks," but rather he maintained that marijuana served a higher purpose. Indeed, during his time back at Columbia, he was studying the paintings of Paul Cézanne, and found that marijuana helped him appreciate and understand the work. This interest in European art would continue to grow and become a great motivating force behind his eventual trips to Europe.

Sadly, after a few weeks back home, he was given the option to sign for his mother's lobotomy. It was a difficult decision, but the doctors convinced him it was the only course of action, and he agreed to it. His parents had divorced, and so it was Allen's responsibility, not his father's, to make this choice. The procedure was devastating for his mother, and Allen never forgave himself for signing the papers. It would haunt him for the rest of his life.

In July, 1948, Allen was lying on his bed at home in Harlem, masturbating and reading William Blake, when he had a vision. He truly believed that he'd seen god, and had no qualms about telling everyone he knew. Just about everyone thought that he'd gone mad, including his analyst, his father, and his professors. His actions and letters from the previous year had shown a man virtually on the edge of his sanity—or at least so it seemed by the stuffy standards of the era—and now he seemed finally to have followed his mother into the realm of the insane. What really happened shall remain unclear, but for Ginsberg it was one of the most important moments of his life, and biographer Barry Miles seemed to credit that experience with much of what happened later:

> Thus he ultimately began a series of experiments with mind-altering drugs, which would continue for fifteen years. . . He disappeared into the upper reaches of the Amazon to take ayahuasca with the Indian witch-doctors and smoked hashish all night with naked sadhus in the burning grounds on the banks of the Ganges.[58]

What Miles is suggesting is that Ginsberg's frantic exploration of interior and exterior space, including his extensive world travels, can be pinned down to this one moment in 1948. Indeed, Ginsberg himself agreed: "I stupefied myself from 1948 to 1963. A long time. That's fifteen years preoccupied with one single thought."[59]

First Trip to Mexico

Ginsberg spent most of 1948 at home in his Harlem apartment or at his dad's house in Paterson. His eyes were on the world, paying attention to news from Asia and obsessing over art from Europe, namely Cézanne, whose paintings he hoped to emulate in poetry. Yet, in spite of his life-changing summer vision of Blake, he was not actually writing all that much poetry. "I am able to write more easily," he wrote Lionel Trilling, "but I still have not found a subject and form and won't for a great while I think."[60] He was working for the Associated Press, doing a nightshift, trying for a while to lead a straight life, but he hated it: "My job is terrible, it leads nowhere. I sure made a compromise with society."[61]

By June, 1949, miserable with his boring life in New York, Ginsberg and Kerouac were planning an exciting journey, an escape from the tedium of regular life. They were either going to take a Huckleberry Finn-style rafting trip down the Mississippi River or else hitch-hike down that more or less same route. The end destination was the new Burroughs residence in New Orleans, where he'd moved after Texas. Ginsberg was determined to "escape" to Louisiana; however, soon Burroughs was arrested for narcotics possession, putting an end to the plan. Worse still, Burroughs' house was searched by the police and Ginsberg's address was on their correspondence. At this time, a number of petty criminals were living with Allen and using his apartment to store their haul. Allen convinced them to move the goods, but the next day, with a stolen car full of stolen merchandise, the police attempted to pull them over. The resulting pursuit ended in a crash. Ginsberg escaped unharmed, but he was later arrested after the police found his papers.

Following the arrest, Ginsberg ended up at the Columbia Presbyterian Psychiatric Hospital, where he met the next important figure in his life, Carl Solomon, to whom Ginsberg later dedicated his most famous poem, "Howl." Though he was two years younger than Allen, Solomon seemed, like all the influential figures in his life to date—Carr, Kerouac, Burroughs, Cassady—more worldly. He had lived in France, where he heard Antonin Artaud perform, and introduced Allen to the work of Artaud, Henri Michaux, and Jean Genet.

The doctors at the Psychiatric Institute soon had Allen thinking he needed to conform to the straight life—including heterosexual relationships—in order to recover, and by 1950 he was dating a young woman named Helen Parker, while working as a reporter. He seemed very happy with this state of affairs, although getting up north to Provincetown, Massachusetts, where she lived, was troublesome. Meanwhile, south of the border, his friends were continuing their less conventional lifestyles. Burroughs had moved to Mexico City after finding the rigid laws of the United States too confining, and he had been joined temporarily by Kerouac and Cassady. Although Burroughs and Ginsberg were not presently seeing eye-to-eye due to Burroughs' disgust at Allen's attempts to go straight, Kerouac was proving to be a loyal and supportive friend.

It was a productive year, at least in terms of poetry, and Ginsberg was moving towards a more recognizable voice, particularly with the influence of Christopher Smart, whose long lines were one of the most important influences on "Howl." In "Paterson," written during 1949, Ginsberg laments being stuck at home and leading a conventional life, toiling for money every day. His real vocation, he says, is back out in the world. He peppers the poem with references to his travels and exploits:

I would rather go mad, gone down the dark road
        to Mexico, heroin dripping in my veins,
        eyes and ears full of marijuana,
eating the God peyote on the floor of a mud hut
        on the border
or laying in a hotel room over the body of some
        suffering man or woman
rather jar my body down the road, crying by a
        diner in the western sun;
rather crawl on my naked belly over the tincans
        of Cincinnati;
rather drag a rotten railroad tie to a Golgotha in
        the Rockies;
rather, crowned with thorns in Galveston, nailed
        hand in foot in Los Angeles, raised up to
        die in Denver,[62]

It is a stark change from the poetry he had written only a few years before, which showed a young man too fearful to venture out into the world.

"Paterson" ends with him "by the bayou and forest and derricks leaving my flesh and my bones hanging on the trees." All of these images of suffering, he says, are worthwhile and are preferable to sitting at home in Paterson or making money at some pointless job.

After jumping from girl to girl and job to job, by the time mid-1951 arrived, Allen had neither a full-time girlfriend nor full-time employment, and he was free to make his next long voyage. For several years he had been confined to the old stomping grounds of New York and New Jersey, with a few excursions up to Massachusetts. Lucian Carr had been living the clean, sensible life longer than Ginsberg, having attempted to stay out of trouble after being released from prison, but he now planned a road trip to Mexico, where one of his friends, Russ Lafferty, was about to get married. He was eager for two wild weeks of fun, just like the old days, before he returned to his job at United Press International. He originally planned to go with Kerouac, but Jack was sick with phlebitis and so Carr asked Allen, who had recently come into a bit of money thanks to a tax refund, to come along.

Burroughs had moved to Mexico in October, 1949, and had sent various letters to his friends back home. Initially, they were enthusiastic. He tried to coax Kerouac down with promises of cheap alcohol—in fact, everything there was cheap. Mexico was different, he said, from the U.S. because people minded their own business and a man could get whatever he wanted with a little bit of money, including drugs and sex with young men. This sounded perfect to Allen, who was also keen on catching up with his old friend.

In late August, the pair set off on the long journey south from New York, via Texas, to Mexico City in Lucian's car—an old Chevrolet—loaded down with alcohol, and Lucian's dog Potchkie in the back seat. Carr drove because Ginsberg couldn't— in fact, despite a few informal lessons, he never learned how to drive. This was Ginsberg's longest single trip by land, at more than 2,500 miles. Passing through a heatwave in Texas, the car's thermometer exploded.

In Mexico City, they planned on staying with

Burroughs, but by the time they arrived he had taken off for Ecuador with Lewis Marker, his boyfriend. Burroughs could be happy with Joan, but once he had his eyes on another man, he was no longer interested in women. He'd left Joan and their two children alone in a Mexico City slum, which is where Allen and Lucian found them. They immediately noted how much Joan had deteriorated under the weight of her alcohol and Benzedrine intake. Between substance abuse and a bout of polio suffered in Texas, she had become a ghost of her original self, and it would seem to Ginsberg, after later events, that she had given up on life and wanted to die.

In Mexico City, perhaps for the first time, Ginsberg played the role of tourist. If one is to distinguish between tourists and travellers, then he had been the latter on several occasions now—to Denver, to Dakar, and so forth. However, he had probably never been a real tourist before, concerned with sightseeing and souvenir-purchasing. In Mexico City, Lucian and Joan got exceptionally drunk together, while Allen went off to see the city, guidebook in hand.

Drinking was to be the theme of this first visit to Mexico, and it even landed Carr in jail once again when he drunkenly crashed his car after delivering the married couple to the airport. Undeterred by that misadventure, he, Allen, and Joan, along with Joan's children, took off for Guadalajara and the Pacific coastline on a drunken search for marijuana. On the trip there, Joan and Lucian took turns driving while Allen and the kids huddled in the back, terrified as the car whipped around hairpin bends and raced along mountain roads. Sometimes Carr was too drunk to focus on the road, so Joan would drive, with Carr lying on the floor, helping her with the pedals because her polio-crippled leg was unable to work both the gas and the brake. Ginsberg thought that Joan was trying to kill herself and take the rest of them with her. Then the car became stuck in a river and some locals came to help them get it out. However, the Mexicans stole Allen's pants, which he'd taken off to avoid getting wet as he pushed the car.

The trip, while terrifying, was also enjoyable and exciting at times. On their wild car ride they had breath-taking views of the Pacific Ocean and Sierra Madre mountains, and they even got close to an active volcano. At Paricutin, they drove onto the lava field at night and attempted to get as close as possible to the volcano itself. The car kept getting stuck and they had to work it out of crevices with the jack. They got within a mile of the rim, where dust and rocks fell, and they could see molten lava cast high into the night sky. Elsewhere, they saw the Pyramid of the Sun and watched bullfights, and agreed that the scenery in the west of the country was the most beautiful in the world.

Years later, Allen recalled "the greatest vision of the earth I ever had" (excluding his Blake vision) as a particular section of their car journey:

> . . . the great rolling plain of Spain between Tepic and Guadalajara, just a few miles outside of Tepic—we rolled down the

vast slope in sunset, the biggest grassy plain I ever saw, coming down from the mountains, long masses of clouds hanging midway between earth and sky, you could see over the clouds we were on slope, and saw little lost city Tepic huddled in the distance.[63]

When it was time to return, Carr was particularly sad to leave, having grown very close to Joan during their drunken time together. The two men began the long car journey home to New York, but in Galveston, Texas, the car broke down. Carr was in a hurry to get back to work, and so he flew home, leaving Ginsberg with his car and the dog. He would return four days later to resume the drive back to New York. In the meantime, Allen rented a small shack overlooking the Gulf of Mexico, and spent his time swimming, sitting on the beach, and exploring Galveston. He'd been there before, albeit very briefly, when his ship passed through on its way from Freeport to Dakar.

On 7th September, he opened the newspaper to read that Burroughs had shot and killed Joan in a drunken game.

Reflections on Part One

In the first part of this book, we have looked at the development of Irwin Allen Ginsberg from a precocious youth who never travelled more than one hundred miles from home during the first nineteen years of his life—and even then only with his family—to a young adult shipping out to Africa on his own, wandering the backstreets of Dakar in search of hard drugs and harder sex, and making his first trip to that most important of Beat Generation locations, Mexico. His motivations for travel were numerous: there was an ever-present curiosity about the world, spurred by his formal and informal educations; there was a personal search for meaning and self-discovery—the internal voyage overlapping with the external; there was an essential drive to make money for school and for therapy—"financial necessity," as biographer Bill Morgan put it; there was lust and love; there was the influence of others, from his older, more experienced friends to fantastic voyages in art and literature; and, ultimately, there was an absolute, blinding sense of despair and loneliness that compelled him to leave the United States. As of mid-1948, we can note another reason that would guide his future travels, and that was the desire to replicate his Blake vision, or at least to better understand what it meant.

The young kid who shipped out to make money and delve deeper into his own psyche by going on a physical voyage at sea, and who set out for the West on his own in a hopeless quest for love, quickly developed the skills to get by outside of his comfort zone. Granted, most of his journeys thus far had been on ships where he had to work and adhere to a routine, but he was learning how to survive away from home, learning how to be a "regular guy," learning how to live on no money and communicate with people from entirely different backgrounds, and in the coming years, which we will explore in Part Two, he would continue to learn how to survive on the road for weeks, months, and years at a time. He was developing language skills that would allow him to speak easily with the people he met on the road, and he had become, in the words of a secretary, many years later, "a terrific map-reader,"[64] able to navigate unfamiliar places. Of particular importance, however, is that we are witnessing the development not just of a young man, but of one of the most important poets in American history, and travel was giving him not just the opportunity to sit down and write, but breakthroughs in his poetry. His work was metamorphosing from derivative, uninspired rhymed verse to something more original, and in the next section of the book we will see how travel helped create some of the greatest poetry in American history, setting him absolutely free from the constraints of the past.

Part Two:
Mastering the Art of Travel
1952-1960

"I think I could go anywhere practically."

In this section of the book, we will explore the most significant and extensive journeys of Allen Ginsberg's life. Here, we will begin to gloss over shorter trips and most domestic travels to instead focus upon the journeys that were significant in his development as a poet and in building a global awareness that would shape him into a prominent countercultural leader of the sixties.

The Long Road to California

After returning from Mexico, Ginsberg spent the next two years in New York City. He was still leading a somewhat straight life, living with girlfriends and working regular jobs, although his homosexual leanings began to return. He was starting to feel an urge to make an "Amazon voyage"[1] and also waiting for the opportunity to ship out again. He was also contemplating a move to Paris or Venice with Kerouac. He felt left out as his friends explored Mexico and the American West, and "tied down yet by ideal of doctors."[2] However, although it attracted him, he was still afraid of heading out into the wider world. In May, 1952, a long letter from Kerouac describing his wild adventures in Mexico both excited and terrified Allen:

> I can't come to Mexico because I am terrified of going off into the night again, toward death maybe, or oblivion beyond the pale tenderness of New York daily life . . . Your letter was monumental and

frightening to me, I wanted immediately to come on down, just like you said, happily and gaily, but instead of kicks under control I am afraid of bum kicks of police, penniless, ragged days.[3]

He recalled his own trip to Mexico fondly, but also remembered "torment of continual death," and said he would only return to travel after he had sufficient funds to allow him a sense of security.

In William Carlos Williams, he finally found a poetry teacher who could give him proper guidance, and taking advice from the old doctor—as well as Kerouac, who remained influential—Ginsberg went back through his journals from the past few years and culled poetry from the entries. As mentioned in the previous section, "The Bricklayer's Lunch Hour" was formed from a hybrid of Kerouac's sketching method and Williams' advice regarding poetic form. Years later, Ginsberg commented that "This is probably the earliest text I published which makes real sense."[4] Indeed, prior to that, his poetry was dense and filled with confusing imagery based upon private mythology, not to mention archaic language. Now, his poetry began to lose the "doths" and "thous" and "thees." As he worked on his poetry in New York, he began to move away from the influence of his father, Van Doren, and Trilling, and towards his own voice, which Gordon Ball referred to as "reality notation."[5]

Another influence developed while in New York—Asian culture. For years, Allen had been interested in paintings, mostly by European artists. At the end of April, 1953, he became obsessed with Chinese and Japanese painting while visiting the Fine Art room at the New York Public Library. He spent days studying these ancient works, presumably drawn to the use of simple lines and negative space, which would have corresponded to the method of poetry he was currently developing under the advice of Williams. He was also undergoing a first round of interest in Buddhism, to which Kerouac introduced him, reading D.T. Suzuki's *Introduction to Zen Buddhism*, along with another seventy titles withdrawn from the Columbia University library. In the concept of satori, he found similarities to his Blake vision of 1948, and in wandering Chinese poets he found a correlation with his footloose Beat Generation contemporaries. Looking further into Asian art and literature, he went as far as to read eight or nine translations of Lao Tse in order to better understand it. His studies led him to a scroll painting which he particularly enjoyed, called "Sakyamuni Coming Out From The Mountain," by Liang Kai, and he wrote a poem inspired by it, using Williams' triadic form. This was not the first time he'd written a poem based upon a painting. He had also done this with Paul Cézanne's "L'Estaque." Nor was any of this the beginning of his interest in Asia and its art and culture, but it marks a significant increase in its importance in his life, as he looked east with respect for the "sublimity and sophistication" of this mysterious, ancient culture.[6]

Another parallel with the Chinese poets was the idea of having friends in distant places, as over this period, although he had friends in New York, many of them were moving to California and elsewhere. Burroughs was touring South America again and Carr was now in the Caribbean. Kerouac was out west with Cassady, and they encouraged Allen to join them. He responded that he was "terrified" of joining them out there.[7] A new acquaintance, Gregory Corso, had departed for the West Coast, too, after quickly growing close to Allen in New York. Although he put it off, determined to stay in New York and continue his therapy, become normal, and develop his poetry further, it seemed inevitable that Allen would be drawn westwards. Bill Morgan remarks in his biography that Allen "longed for adventure" at this point.[8] He was also looking to continue his investigation into Asian art and culture in California.

The final push came when Burroughs returned and developed an intense love for Ginsberg, which frightened the younger poet, and in November, 1953, he hastened previously stalled plans for a new journey—one which would become the most important of his life thus far. He decided it was time to move out west with his friends, but he planned on taking a bizarrely circuitous route via Mexico. As is clear from the previous chapter, and would become clearer after this trip, Mexico was already holding a particular allure for Allen, and he was keen to explore further before reaching California. He explained to Cassady:

> This is a rare and marvelous trip I need
> to feed (and free) my soul from ten years
> of NYC which I can afford to make—and

as you must agree, should make, so when
I see you I'll be able to talk for hours, not
only about NYC intellectual beauties, but
also manly savage solitude of jungles we've
never seen—will add to our store of souls.[9]

It is clear that he wanted to build upon his development in the previous few years, perhaps applying his poetic and intellectual abilities to an entirely new landscape and culture. The phrase "manly savage solitude of jungles" is not only characteristic of Ginsberg's developing poetic phrasing (he had recently begun eliminating articles), but reveals a desire to break from his urban environment, to get away from New York intellectualism and comfortable western life, and escape into a more natural environment that offered an entirely different human experience. He makes it sound exciting and romantic, yet it was not entirely intended as a respite from intellectual pursuit. He viewed himself as a poet-explorer in the vein of Byron and intended to see the Mayan ruins—some of which had only recently been discovered—and take inspiration from these as Byron had done with the relics of Athens and Rome.

To pay for the trip he borrowed money from his brother, Eugene, and some friends. He got back-pay from his job, claimed the security deposit on his apartment, and sold his refrigerator. Altogether, he saved $300, part of which he forwarded to the Cassadys for safe-keeping. However, the trip was to be fraught with financial difficulties, and overcoming these was an incredibly important experience for Allen, giving him the skills to survive on his own, away from home, for extended periods of time.

In December, Burroughs departed for Tangiers, where he was to spend most of the fifties, and on the nineteenth, Allen took off, oddly, for Burroughs' parents' house in Florida. He hitch-hiked down the East Coast of the U.S., stopping off firstly in Washington D.C. to view the Freer Collection of oriental paintings, then in Jacksonville, Florida, where he met Lewis Marker, with whom he no doubt shared stories of being the object of Burroughs' warped affections. Years later, he recalled that the only part of Florida that was of any interest to him was the "Negro district" in Jacksonville.[10] Marker gave him some money towards his trip, and he continued on to Palm Beach, where he spent Christmas with the Burroughses, who kindly paid for his hotel and drove him around as he did some sight-seeing. He visited a friend in "horrid Miami Beach,"[11] which he called "a dream of rich sick Jews,"[12] staying at a hotel for $1.50, before heading south to Key West in the back of a truck. Key West, he thought, was "pretty like Provincetown,"[13] although he was not hugely impressed by it, and from there took a $10 boat ride to Havana.

Cuba was in the midst of an especially turbulent period in its history when Ginsberg arrived. The Cuban Revolution had begun some six months prior to Allen's arrival as Fidel and Raúl Castro launched a military attack intended to overthrow the government. It was, however, initially crushed as its leaders were jailed and Fulgencio Batista remained in charge of the country, so when Allen arrived he found himself in a country with a dictator controlling the land through a brutal police force. This was the third foreign country he'd visited, after French West Africa and Mexico, and he had high hopes.* For some reason, he was confident that he would stumble upon vast orgies in Havana, but instead he found it rather tame. Perhaps its perilous political situation had put a stop to the orgies, or perhaps Ginsberg was being fanciful in his imagination as he had been with his trip to Africa some years earlier. Cuba did have a reputation among some Americans for its permissive attitudes to gambling, drinking, and prostitution, and much of this persisted even through the turbulent fifties. Allen stayed at the Carabanchel Hotel in Havana, during which time he did a lot of drinking and sightseeing. He wrote to Kerouac and the Cassadys in California about "horrid Havana":

> Havana I won't talk of—kind of dreary rotting antiquity rotting stone, heaviness all about and don't dig Cubans much even in Cuba. Got lost penniless 20 miles out of town in small village and had to be sent home on train with man who bought me drinks. So sad, so hospitable, but I wanted to get away can't dig his fate.[14]

In Cuba, he wrote what he later referred to as

---

* As I can find no hard evidence of his having visited Cameroon (then French Equatorial Africa), I shall exclude it from the count.

"a minor poem" called "Havana 1953." It would be published ten years later in his collection, *Reality Sandwiches*, along with some other travel-inspired poems. Although it has largely been overlooked by scholars, Ginsberg considered it worthy of reading into the seventies, and he even taught it on his poetry course at Naropa to help his students understand the development of his poetic style. Although one can see earlier examples of a hybridisation of Kerouac's and Williams' influence, it's worth noting that this is the poem to which Ginsberg himself pointed as fusing those two influences into his own voice. He called it his "1953 imitation of Kerouac's sketches put into Williams's relative measured triadic line."[15] The poem begins with Ginsberg sketching his surroundings, per Kerouac's suggestion, and is broken into sets of three lines arranged visually rather than by breath, resulting in a vivid portrait of night time Havana:

> The night café—4 A.M.
>   Cuba Libre 20c:
>   White tiled squares
>   triangular neon lights,
>   long wooden bar on one side,
>   a great delicatessen booth[16]

Another poetic influence at this point, and perhaps an inspiration for his particular route to California, was Hart Crane. As we saw in Part One, Ginsberg had been pleased to find himself in the Gulf of Mexico during his Merchant Marine days, on "Hart Crane seas." In his journals, around 1952, he began copying Crane's use of the dash as punctuation during passages of extended description. While teaching at Naropa in the seventies, he assigned his students Crane's "Voyages" and mentioned the importance of "Havana Rose" on his own poetry:

> . . . it was one of the things which turned me on to raw thought as poetry, a little free-associational piece, like the kind of note you might write to yourself drunk which wasn't meant as a poem . . . [17]

In his journals from the coming Mexican trip, and journeys beyond that through Europe and Asia, the impact of Crane is clear in his quick flourishes of detail, built up to create layer upon layer of striking images amidst his thoughts.

It seems, from his journals and letters, that this trip marks a stage in his writing where Ginsberg begins to look outwards at the world, whereas previously his work had been marked by intense introspection, often filled with self-criticisms, or descriptions and analyses of dreams. The combination of influences—Kerouac, Williams, Crane, and even the painter Cézanne—conspired to bring about a style of work wherein Ginsberg became concerned with capturing the world around him. In letters and journal entries, his prose is often disjointed, jumping from place to place, offering fragmentary images, but these images are vivid and build up a whole picture. Ginsberg would later mine his journals for these details and piece them together into effective poetry. Although he had been "mining" (his phrase) for a few years, and had practiced some form of sketching as early as 1948, these methods really began coming together effectively with his great travels of 1953-54.

Mexico

He was relieved when he departed Cuba for Mexico. The flight from Havana to Mérida, the capital of the Yucatán peninsula, was his first time on an airplane, and he very much enjoyed the experience:

> Marvelous first airplane air vistas of the earth, Carib Isles, great green maplike Yucatan Coast maplike below with sink-holes in earth of limestone crust and narrow road and trails like antpath down below and little cities like mushrooms in pockets and hollows of afternoon hills, and windmills.[18]*

He arrived in Mérida, where he planned to stay for three days, early in the morning on 31st December. In what would become typical Ginsberg fashion, he somehow bumped into some locals (Quintana

---

* Several decades later, he was still enamored of air travel, saying an airline seat "is great meditative poetic place where you can't do anything but sit and look out through heaven"

Roo Indians) and was taken on a horse-drawn cart around the city, during which time he somehow met the mayor's brother and was invited to the City Hall New Year's Eve celebrations. He soon found himself at a fancy party, surrounded by elite types "in blue lace dresses, and stark black and white or pink grand costumes," drinking free beer and champagne. "I was not prepared in my travels to meet such a profound manifestation of wealth and style," he wrote in his journal, while humorously lamenting having not brought a tuxedo on his hitch-hiking venture into the jungle.[19] After the party he went downtown to the poorer districts and listened to mambo in clubs until 5am. He was clearly more at home among the poor than the rich, and he seemed uncomfortable when the next day he was back at City Hall to listen to the Mayor's New Year's Day address, which Ginsberg claims went on for an hour and a half as the rich folk sat idly sipping their iced drinks.

Later, he travelled to Chichén Itzá, where he pretended to be an archaeology student in order to stay for free in a house next to the pyramid. A contact made through the Museum of Natural History in New York had given him a student pass, allowing him to stay for free anywhere in Mexico with an archaeological camp. During the day, he socialized with the archaeologists and tourists, but at night he was on his own. His first night there, at about eight o'clock, he took Paracodeina (an opiate) and climbed up El Castillo—the giant Mayan pyramid—with a hammock, and spent an hour under the stars. He wrote to his friends in California:

. . . spent days eating in native hut for $7 pesos a day wandering around great ruins—at nite take hammock up on top of big pyramid temple . . . and look at stars and void and deathheads engraved up on stone pillars and write and doze on codeinetta.[20]

He continues, describing the "chirruping insects" and hooting of owls. Many of the ideas and even exact phrases he uses are repeated in his journal, providing vivid descriptions of the sky, the forest, and the ruins around him. Some of this later found its way into his great Mexican poem, "Siesta in Xbalba and Return to the States," which we will return to later. The "deathsheads" that he mentions above are described in more detail in his journal, and refer to skulls carved into bas-reliefs, which Ginsberg thought of as "portals."[21] As he looked into the eye sockets of the skull carvings, he felt himself connecting to the ancient artisan who originally created the work, and saw the passing of centuries as the stone was worn down. Yet although impressed by the Mayan ruins that he had come to Mexico to see, he appears more impressed by nature, and much of his writing reflects this connection to the natural world. After an hour atop the great pyramid, he had a vision of his mother when she was young, "in rapport with life."[22]

His journals are filled with dense notes on the architecture of the Mayan ruins he found throughout Mexico, with Chichén Itzá of course being the most interesting. Often, he seemed taken by the sounds of the buildings at night. He said of Chichén Itzá, "the main kick was the wild acoustics—somewhere in the middle of all these buildings is a place where you can clap your hands and be heard in heaven."[23]

Despite having gotten so much for free during his first days in Mexico, Ginsberg's money was already running low as he moved towards Valladolid. In the mid-twentieth century, Valladolid was a comparatively affluent city, and one of the most important in the Yucatán. There, Ginsberg stayed with an English-speaking man in "his middleclass family house," where he ate with the family.[24] The man showed Ginsberg around "the tower," referring to the Cathedral de San Servasio—a Spanish cathedral that was built from stones the Spaniards took from Mayan temples five hundred years earlier.

The next day, 6th January, he took off at 4am on a cramped train ride headed for Tizimín (a "really crowded small town in the middle of nowhere"), to see "the oldest fiesta of Mexico," by which he meant Three Kings Day.[25] The awful train ride lasted ten hours, with a hundred people per train car, and at one point it came off the rails. His journal entry for this day, whilst descriptive, shows he was frustrated and uncomfortable, with little patience for the experience. He heard from another American visitor that the filmmaker Paul Rotha was in town, shooting a documentary. This refers to the UNESCO-sponsored World Without End, shot in Mexico and Thailand.

At the Tizimín cathedral, Ginsberg met a priest who drove him to his village in the jungle, where they stayed the night before exploring the area together the following day. Then the priest took him to the train station, where he set off on another insufferable ten-hour journey back to Valladolid on 12th January. Thankfully, he was able to spend another enjoyable day and night at Chichén Itzá to recover from the unpleasant train experience, and from there returned to Mérida with just $25 in his pocket.

Ginsberg's famous networking skills were improving greatly throughout this journey, and everywhere he went he seemed to meet people who could help him out with food, shelter, directions, and other advice. Although he had largely been able to get by speaking English or French to people, he was learning some Spanish. By now he had picked up enough of the language to communicate his basic needs, but he was making mistakes in communication that were costing him money. For example, he once purchased the wrong kind of hammock and lost nine pesos.

His next stop was another ancient and important Mayan city—Uxmal, located a little over sixty kilometres south of Mérida. He had been overwhelmed by the magnificence of Chichén Itzá, but Uxmal, he thought, was even more impressive. His journals are filled with vivid descriptions, some of which are in an almost Kerouacian sketch style. He was fascinated by the labyrinthine paths running through the jungle between parts of the ancient city. Sometimes he would go out exploring and end up back where he started completely by accident, and other times he would stumble upon something entirely new. The ground was littered with fragments of pottery and stone hinting at stories from centuries ago. In high school and university, he had been awed by the wonders of classical Europe, and in 1952-53 he had begun to look east and marvel at the "sublimity and sophistication" of ancient Asian societies, but now he noted: "I'd never realized the vast sophistication of Pre-Columbian America."[26]

On 15th January, his last day at Uxmal, he took codeine again and described the scene at sunset using long lines that seem to be further developing his poetic technique from Kerouac-inspired sketching (with Crane-like punctuation) into a use of breath to form long sentences more like Smart, which would be most famously utilised in his *magnum opus*, "Howl."

> In walking shoes and army pants & Mérida
> hat seated at ease atop the highest mount
> to see & rest—6:30 must soon descend—
> always a little afraid of these steep stairs—
> and eat at Bar and Restaurant last meal at
> Uxmal—the grand Quinque burning with
> loud rushing air noise casting brilliant
> whitelike-sunlite lite on the driveway so as
> snow looks: Smoking Otros.[27]

He noted in another journal entry that same day that "only the intensest writing is interesting," requiring a careful mix of surface details and "soul river thought."[28] He was already making huge progress in forming his own poetic voice.

From Uxmal, Ginsberg travelled through Campeche

to the Mayan City of Palenque, in the interior of Mexico. Much smaller than Chichén Itzá or Uxmal, it is nonetheless an important archaeological site, and significant discoveries had been made not long before Allen's arrival in 1954. Even today, only a fraction of the city has been uncovered, and when Ginsberg visited it seemed like a true lost city, having been consumed by the jungle long before the Spanish arrived in the Americas. Once again, he vividly described what he saw from various vantage points, comparing the scene to Chinese paintings he had studied in New York. He also practiced his sketching by the light of the full moon, focusing on sounds rather than images. With each day, his writing style developed into more carefully condensed images.

Here in Palenque, Ginsberg had vivid dreams about being in Europe among the "ancient parapets."* This was not the first time in Mexico that he had been carried off to Europe in his imagination. In his dreams he abandoned his life in America and set off on a ship across the Atlantic. In one, he found himself on a train through Italy with Burroughs. Afterwards, he was further convinced that he needed to visit Europe one day, a feeling that grew throughout his time in Mexico, and expanded beyond Europe to ancient ruins of cultures across the globe, as far off as Ankara and Angkor Wat. At Chichén Itzá he had been sad that his

---

* This is likely a reference to Arthur Rimbaud: "I long for Europe of the ancient parapets!" Fifteen years later he noted another dream like the one he had in Mexico, and in his journal he used the same phrase: "ancient parapets."

journey would end back in America, when what he wanted was to continue on to Europe, writing about everything he saw. Biographer, Barry Miles, speculated that "The Mayan ruins had evoked a desire to see the antiquities of his own culture,"[29] yet whilst there is some truth to this, Ginsberg was partly in Mexico to do the opposite—to view the heritage of this continent the same way other poets viewed classical Europe:

> While I was in Chichén Itzá and Palenque, cities of the old Maya empire on the Yucatán peninsula, I thought that [it] would be interesting to treat them as if they were the great ruins of Greece that Shelley and Keats wrote about. Why couldn't the Americans use those Central American ruins for the same nostalgia and classical reference, the same sense of the eternal, time in eternity?[30]

Although he had arrived in Palenque in a bad mood due to a handful of persistent illnesses and his perpetual lack of funds, Ginsberg was greatly cheered up when he met Karena Shields, an archaeologist working on the site. She had been in Chiapas since she was three years old, when her father brought her over from the United States to live on a rubber plantation. She told Allen that the indigenous population, the Karivís, knew ancient Mayan secrets, which had been passed down over the centuries. This seemed to resonate with Ginsberg, who had been introduced to Mayan history by Burroughs, whose interpretation of Mayan language and culture was somewhat supernatural. Allen spoke of Shields in his letters to friends with a sense of admiration that he rarely reserved for women, passing along stories of her childhood, her archaeological discoveries, and her intellect.

Ginsberg got along so well with Shields that she invited him to stay on her plantation, deep in the jungle of Chiapas. Naturally, Allen accepted. Here, at *Finica Tacalapán de San Leandro*, he found true solitude. It was a seven-hour trip by jeep and horse (his first time on horseback) through dense jungle, and at the plantation there was only Allen, Karena, and local Indians. Although invited only for a week, he spent several months there, mostly lounging about and writing. He had done a lot of writing during his time in Mexico, but mostly it was short journal entries and letters sketching scenes from the ruins he visited. In a relatively short space of time, he had covered a lot of ground from Mérida to Palenque, but now it was time for him to lie back in his hammock, amidst the sounds of the jungle, and work on his poetry and "let the mind wander into its solitude & vacancy with the sheer idea of finding an ungraspable spirit."[31] He grew out his beard and hair for the first time, beginning to look like the image of Allen Ginsberg that would be so famous during the 1960s and beyond.

It was his prophesy of "manly savage solitude of jungles" come true. Deep in the jungle, the city boy washed away the New York grime and learned to survive in a place that may as well have been a million miles from the nearest supermarket or bank. At night he went fishing under the stars and even once saw "a perfect lunar eclipse."[32] By day he speared crawfish with sticks, swam naked in the river, built and played giant drums, farmed bananas and cocoa, and trekked alone into the dark and dangerous jungle. He noted in his letters that people came to the plantation with snakebites and gunshot wounds in search of medical assistance, and he watched in fascination as they were patched up by Shields. He still had time to lie around in his hammock for hours, "conceiving a familiar uncanny sensation which never comes to me whole, presumably too divine," and even pondered becoming a monk.[33] Yet such was the solitude afforded him that he also had time to spend between five and ten hours each day just working on his poetry.

The most important work to emerge from this period of isolation was "Siesta in Xbalba and Return to the States,"* the first half of which was written on the plantation. This poem was briefly mentioned earlier in this book for containing references to his observations at Chichén Itzá, as he was mining his journals and letters for ideas, images, and phrases he could incorporate into his poetry. Although he frequently used his notebooks as material for his poetry, "Siesta in Xbalba" is rather extreme in that he takes many phrases from throughout the whole of his travels in Mexico. The poem begins with a juxtaposition of his

---

* Xbalba is a misspelling of Xibalba, which refers to the underworld of Mayan mythology.

present situation—lying in a hammock in the jungle—against the intrusion of the possibility of a return to his former life. The jungle situation seems idyllic, and the city appears chaotic and superficial. It begins:

> ... —One could pass valuable months
> and years perhaps a lifetime
> doing nothing but lying in a hammock
> reading prose with the white doves
>   copulating underneath
> and monkeys barking in the interior
>   of the mountain
> and I have succumbed to this
>   temptation—...[34]

The first part of the poem offers rich descriptions of his time in Mexico, with the various locations acting as a composite place—Xbalba. It is starkly contrasted with images of New York, and Mexico appears almost magical by comparison. Even his 1948 vision, which is briefly mentioned, pales when compared to sitting atop a pyramid or walking in the jungle. The second part is much shorter, and details his return to the United States. (This section was written in California after his return.) However, it is not entirely bleak. He returns wiser and more capable of leading his life. His eyes were open and he could view America more clearly.

On the plantation, Ginsberg also wrote his second ever song, "Green Valentine Blues." It shows that, although he was generally happy in Mexico, he was also lonely and wondering if he would ever find love. He later said, "'Green Valentine' echoes some old Tin Pan Alley, music hall barbershop, almost vaudeville number, sentimental like 'My Yiddishe Mama,' the kind of thing you sing to yourself in bed . . ."[35] At the time of writing the song, he was also working on his drumming, playing giant jungle drums, and claimed, "my smooth easy-to-dance-to style is a great wonder."[36] With his goatee and bongo set, he was prefiguring the beatnik trend of the late fifties.

At the beginning of February, the residents of the plantation witnessed a bright meteor race across the sky, which was followed by an immense tremor that shook the buildings and made the hammocks swing. After a few weeks, Ginsberg was getting restless and curious about the rumours that were passing through the jungle regarding the tremor. Some Indians were speculating that a volcano had erupted, killing people in the nearby town of Yajalón and destroying the town's four-hundred-year-old church.

Ginsberg set out to investigate the true story behind the tremor and subsequent rumours. At the nearest village, Salta de Agua, he found a "crazy American" pilot called Captain Cover who would fly him over the jungle to Yajalón in an old plane. This was preferable to a two- or three-day journey through the jungle on a mule. Ginsberg did a lot of research into the area during his short stay at Salta, and described it in detail as a hop-off point into the great unknown of the jungles and mountains of Chiapas and Guatemala. Yet it is also worth noting that in describing Salta he twice refers to it as like China, and like a Cézanne painting—two of his recent obsessions.

He arrived in Yajalón with one hundred pesos, his pen and journal, and nothing else. Here, in this beautiful little old town, he found the old church still standing, although a house may have collapsed near the airfield. Evidently, by the time the story had travelled just a short distance, the jungle had swallowed most of the truth and spat out fiction. Even more confusion abounded—although, one must wonder to what extent that is due to his own translation skills—regarding the local volcano. Was it a volcano or not? Was it active, extinct, or dormant? Ginsberg reported uncertainty in a letter to Kerouac, and placed himself as the man to find the truth.

Viewing himself as a heroic amateur geologist, Ginsberg set out on a borrowed mule for the volcano, which is called Huitepec, despite Allen repeatedly referring to it as Mt Acavalna in his letters and journals.* Allen seemed to like the name, and speculated its meaning in local languages, ultimately deciding that it was "Blakean."[37] Two men from Yajalón followed him, and more joined at each passing village as he headed for the volcano in search of a story. He spent his first night at a small village called Zapata, where the whole world seemed to shake under his feet. The villagers said that it was a regular occurrence. After a

* Ginsberg misspells many locations in Mexico, including this one, in his letters and journals. He later worried that his letters would be "gibberish" to his friends without accompanying maps because he refers to so many place names, but with the benefit of maps it is even more confusing as very few places he mentions exist by those names.

night of violent tremors underfoot, he was regretting his decision to visit the volcano, but by morning he was now the leader of an expedition numbering fifty-four men and his pride outweighed his fears. "Can't tell you how I enjoyed the situation," he told Kerouac. "I was the leader, I organized and supplied the general power and intelligence—and I was deferred to."[38]

At the summit, they found no sign of volcanic eruption (the volcano was extinct), and the tremors remained a mystery. (However, they were almost certainly aftershocks from a major earthquake two months earlier.) They returned to Zapata, where Allen wrote a report for the local towns and villages, as well as the Geological Institute and government. However, before he could set off for Shields' plantation, he was ambushed by Indians who wanted him to lead another expedition—this time to the other side of the volcano, where there used to be a cave. They wanted to know whether or not it had been destroyed by the earthquake. For Ginsberg, it was another chance to play the role of intrepid explorer.

They set off the next morning and discovered a giant cavern that Allen said was "as big as St Patrick's Cathedral."[39] Indeed, after its rediscovery by Allen's expedition, it was studied and confirmed as one of the largest in the hemisphere. He went on to say that he was the "first stranger other than Indians ever there" and that he solved the riddle of the mountain's name, which meant "House of Night." That last part was probably fanciful, but nonetheless Ginsberg was delighted to have led a successful expedition. He told

Kerouac, "It was a real great *Life* magazine intrepid American adventurer situation, I really was a great hero and nobody knew except in Yajalón."[40] He stayed at Yajalón for some time to write up the story for a local newspaper, and while he was there he was treated practically as royalty by the locals, and launched new expeditions into other areas of central Chiapas.

To what extent this story is true, one is unsure. It seems to exist entirely through the journals and letters of Allen Ginsberg. His newspaper article went unpublished, and tracking down any additional information has proven extremely difficult. Nonetheless, even if he made little or no mark on the world of geology, the expedition was tremendously important to Allen. "I became a local hero," he told friends. "The cave was legendary, I was the first to verify it officially." [41] He had set out for Mexico to find "manly savage solitude of jungles" and had done so, becoming manly in his own way. He was, perhaps for the first time in his life, feeling like an alpha male.

After his grand adventure, Allen returned to Shields' plantation with just ten pesos to his name. Having followed in the footsteps of his poet-traveller heroes like Rimbaud it was now time to settle back down at the *finica* and spend some time working on "Siesta in Xbalba." He made a note to research the geology of volcanoes and earthquakes, too, which would be useful now that he considered himself an authority on the subject. He also tried to get back in touch with the outside world, but his letters to Burroughs and others had been lost by the Mexican postal service, and they were all worried about him. The Allen Ginsberg they'd known in New York surely couldn't have survived in the jungles of Mexico for very long. The situation worsened when money sent to Allen disappeared or was returned, and Burroughs was terrified that something awful had happened. His worry was infectious, and he harangued other friends and family to help track Allen down.

At the beginning of May, Allen was stuck in Salta de Agua, waiting for money so that he could get out of the jungle. It was time to move on from Mexico and visit the Cassadys in California as he had originally planned. As he waited, he drank alcohol for the first time in months, watched doctors perform medical procedures on Indians, and dreamed that he had leprosy. He was finally growing tired of the jungle and had an impulse to suddenly escape to Mexico City. Money sent to him by his brother was not enough for him to reach the capital, but eventually he was able to borrow from Shields, who was also nearly broke at this point.

On 13th May, Ginsberg took a train to Coatzacoalcos, commenting upon its "lunar landscape," then an overnight bus to Vera Cruz, and then on to the capital. In Mexico City, he felt sad that everyone he knew there was now gone, especially Joan. He went and stood outside her old house on Orizaba Street, seeing a vision of her walking alone in the street, abandoned by everyone who knew her there. Elsewhere, he wrote short sketches of places around the city—densely packed sentences filled with observations about his surroundings with minimum use of punctuation and grammatical items:

> Sitting crosslegged on concrete walk, dark
> palm at left at right circular glass book
> display window with red & modern signs,
> books & writers in neon lights—to the right
> the sexy park—ahead the unknown Times
> Square Neons of Mexcity—Max Factor,
> Dry Martini, red, green, circular motion of
> moving signs, sound of great city trolleys
> behind, old lady beggar sitting on pave
> near Library.[42]

By 23rd May, he was in Patzcuaro, halfway between
Mexico City and the Pacific Coast, and from there he
travelled north to San Miguel de Allende, where he
had sex for the first time in six months. Prior to this
he had been masturbating frequently, and had grown
tired of his "own crooked selfy cock," lusting after
Indians he saw on buses.[43] From there, he took a bus
to Guanajuato, a wealthy city which produced between
one and two thirds of the world's entire supply of silver.
He described the downtown area in terms that seem
very American compared with the places he'd visited
elsewhere in Mexico, and in marked contrast to his visit
to the recently unearthed mummies, where he shot
photos of their eerily preserved bodies and ruminated
upon the topic of death. He remarked that the smell
"remind[ed] one of sperm and drunkenness."[44]

He continued north through Zacatecas and then
headed west from Durango to Mazatlán, on the Pacific

coast. He had been through that area a few years earlier, with Lucian Carr and Joan Vollmer, noting its astounding natural beauty. He then spent a day sightseeing at Guaymas, before taking the long bus ride north through Magdelena to Mexicali, at the U.S. border. Arriving in Mexicali at the beginning of June, he noted the absolute poverty that existed there, just across the border from the great wealthy United States. After a night on the edge of a slum, he walked across the border and took a Greyhound bus up to Los Angeles, where he stayed with a cousin, before heading to the Cassadys' house in San Jose. It had been a long trip west from New York.

The Voyager Returns a Poet

When Ginsberg returned to the United States in July, 1954, he had been away for more than six months. He was a changed man. Those six months had been filled with new experiences that had challenged him and educated him. No longer was he scared and intimidated by the road and all its experiences as he had been back in 1952 when faced with the prospect of a solo voyage. He claimed to speak Spanish now and some Mayan, and said "I think I could go anywhere practically."[45] The timid intellectual from the big city had survived the darkest jungles and led an expedition into a volcano. He was, in his own mind, a hero. From this point on, he would venture into all the nooks and crannies of the world without the same sense of fear that previously beset his mind.

Perhaps more importantly, though, the experience had opened his eyes and his mind to the world, and begun a process that would continue with his next major journeys—of viewing the United States from an outsider's perspective. Several scholars, including Jonah Raskin, have remarked upon the significance of travelling outside the United States to the development of Beat literature, with Mexico being of particular importance. He explained that "Mexico played a pivotal part in [Allen's] liberation from himself and from America."[46] This allowed the Beats to view themselves and their own culture from a distance, gaining a perspective that was uncommon among their peers. Decades later, Ginsberg called it "the breakthrough of the Beat Generation," noting the importance of realising "the American standard was not the only standard."[47]

Mexico was important for many members of the Beat Generation, and Ginsberg told early Beat scholar John Tytell "that [he] would never fully understand the members of [Ginsberg's] generation until [he] first experienced Mexico." The country had a profound influence over the lives and art of Jack Kerouac and William S. Burroughs, as well as Ginsberg. Years later, when explaining the meaning of Kerouac's On the Road, Ginsberg said that critics didn't get the book from a cultural standpoint, as they were too entrenched in their own provincial American outlook:

Most critics have assumed that there is no point to the book or that there is nothing at the end of the road but blankness. But they get to the end of the road and discover that there's a world outside of America, and a whole vast fellaheen, non-*Time* magazine, nonmechanical, non-petrochemical existence, that escapes the purview of the *New York Times* and the *Washington Post* and the universities and the calculations of academics and mathematicians and politicians and artists.[48]

Soon after his arrival in California, he sat down to write his best-known and arguably his greatest poem, "Howl." Tytell credited the literary breakthrough that allowed Ginsberg to write "Howl" to his experiences in Mexico, calling it a "breakthrough in consciousness"[49] and saying elsewhere:

Living on a plantation in Chiapas, Mexico, became a transformative experience, opening a doorway to the discovery of an authentic new voice. "Howl" was to be its first expression.[50]

Indeed, while "Howl" mostly drew upon his experiences in New York and San Francisco for its content (with some exceptions), his great breakthrough was in the poetic techniques he developed for the poem, which he had cultivated in Mexico. In later years, he picked out

"Havana 1953" and "Siesta in Xbalba" as milestones in his development as a poet, moving from imitations of his greatest poetic influences to his own unique voice. In particular, "Xbalba" was a poem that set him very much on course to write "Howl." In a 1959 letter to a former Columbia classmate, in which Ginsberg defends his work against what he perceives as ignorant criticism, he implies that "Xbalba" was the poem that freed him from previous constraints and led "inevitably and naturally" to the innovation in line creation and "COMPOUND imagism" necessary for "Howl."[51] Jonah Raskin, in *American Scream: Allen Ginsberg's Howl and the Making of the Beat Generation*, noted that even some of the "key words" from "Howl" began to appear in Allen's vocabulary during his time in Mexico and were used in "Xbalba."[52] Even the word "howl" starts to pop up with increasing frequency throughout his journals, letters, and poems from Cuba and Mexico.

It was not just "Howl" that emerged from his Mexican voyage. Back in the U.S., Ginsberg's mind was now freed, and he began to experiment with his poetry more than ever before. He now felt that the "[t]rouble with conventional form (fixed line count and stanza form) is, it's too symmetrical, geometrical, numbered and pre-fixed—unlike to my own mind which has no beginning and end, nor fixed measure of thought."[53] Instead, he was free to mine his mind for ideas and put them on paper in a way that reflected how he felt. The constraints of the past were now gone, and he was free to play with the numerous literary influences he had accumulated. He also now had a wealth of real world experience to weave into his poems. As Michael Schumacher noted, "Ginsberg's travels rewarded him with a profound, mature worldview that added depth to all of his writing."[54]

The first two years that he was back in America were ones of massive literary output and unparalleled inventiveness. One of his most beautiful poems, "Song," was written in San Jose, 1954. Beginning with the oft-quoted line, "The weight of the world/ is love," it marks a sharp departure from his previous work in terms of form and content. It is freer and more playful than previous works, and yet "profound" and "mature" as Schumacher noted. On the surface, it too is rather different from "Howl," yet it acts as a sort of transition. As Raskin noted, certain words entered Ginsberg's lexicon during his time in Mexico, becoming common enough in his mind to permeate his journals, letters, and poems. The word "solitude," which appears frequently in his Mexican writings, is repeated twice in the relatively short "Song," and four times throughout "Howl." Of the opening three lines of "Howl," the words "mad" (from madness), "angel" (from angel-headed), "burning," and "machine" (from machinery) all appear in "Song" as well as in his journals.

Between 1954 and 1956, Ginsberg wrote many of his greatest works, and all of them were borne of the sense of maturity and freedom gained from his Mexican voyage, as well as his newfound ability to "notice what you notice."[55]

Back to Sea

Throughout his time in Mexico, Ginsberg often dreamed of Europe and Asia. During his last month there, he began to think more seriously about his next travels, lamenting that the Mexico trip was coming to an end and that he would soon be back in the U.S. Feeling old now that he was twenty-eight, he recalled "the utter sordidness of my NY worklife," and hoped to soon continue his world travels further afield:

> In Europe I hope to dream about Asia. In Asia I shall dream about the death of Home States. I hope to circumnavigate the globe before the spirit gives out.[56]

It was a remarkably prophetic statement because absolutely everything he mentioned came true, and it also shows that even during his first long foreign voyage he was already planning others. Yet it also refers back to an early influence upon Ginsberg, and something that thus far I have given little credit to as influential upon his desire to see the world—Oswald Spengler's *The Decline of the West*.

Almost a decade earlier, Burroughs had given Kerouac and Ginsberg books from his personal collection, one of which was Spengler's *The Decline of the West*. In Mexico, Ginsberg and Kerouac found validation of Spengler's notion that the poor and uneducated people were the truly great ones, and that they would rightly inherit the earth when the intellectual western world soon fell.* Oddly, throughout his time in Mexico, Ginsberg had described people and places as Chinese, including a mine which made him think of the Great Wall of China because of its vastness. He even compared himself to Chinese labourers in some of his writings. Travelling outside the U.S. seems to have caused him to blend his obsession with the East into his enthusiasm for Spengler, causing him to view large chunks of the world's population as "Fellah."

In any case, within two months of returning to America, Allen was referring to himself as "a wandering Taoist Bum"[57] and claiming to study Buddhism and yoga, expounding upon the virtues of Chinese art and poetry, systematically exploring San Francisco's Chinatown, defending Mao Zedong as a sensitive poet type, and viciously attacking the U.S. government and other western sources of power. He now believed that power was shifting out of western hands, and that it wasn't necessarily a bad thing:

> Just think a few years ago *Life* was talking about the American Century. It's obviously the Asiatic century if it's anybody's. Spengler etc . . . we never had a Chinaman's chance to limit or ignore India, China, Russia, socialism, etc. All we've done is fucked everything up by forcing them to fight us and become as

---

* John Lardas' The Bop Apocalypse is the best discussion of the significance of Spengler on the Beat Generation.

monstrous as we are ... There's an obvious relation between the evils of competitive usury capitalism and the whole senseless self righteous psychology that goes with it and the present fact of our being humbled and beat down by the rest of the world who are plain sick of us. Everybody from Europe to India has been saying that for years and we still haven't caught on.[58]

Although he had been outspoken on political matters as a young man, he had been less vocal on politics for ten years before this return to America. Now that he was back in the U.S., living on the Left Coast, and filled with a new perspective on life he'd gained from wandering south of the border, he was obsessed with his old Spenglerian ideas: "Is the Fall of America already upon us? The Great Fall we once prophesied."[59]

Over the coming years he would often mention to friends his desire to visit Asia, but he wouldn't actually get there until eight years later. In the meantime, he was in San Francisco, where he soon found himself at the centre of major cultural events. His new circle of friends included the poets Philip Whalen and Gary Snyder, who both impressed him with their knowledge of Asia, as well as Peter Orlovsky, with whom Allen would later travel the world. Snyder in particular taught Ginsberg a great deal about Zen Buddhism, and helped put into context the Chinese and Japanese poems and paintings Ginsberg had previously enjoyed. He communicated a lot with Kerouac about Buddhism, but wasn't immediately able to grasp what his friend meant, despite Kerouac's efforts. He complained he was "unfamiliar with [the] vocabulary" Kerouac used and therefore couldn't truly comprehend his friend's advice, but he read extensively in an effort to keep up.[60]

With Whalen, Snyder, and others, Ginsberg put on the legendary Six Gallery poetry reading, at which he gave the first public reading of "Howl," and became an overnight celebrity. Just a few months later, Snyder and Ginsberg took off for the Pacific Northwest, camping in the mountains and hiking across the border into Canada, where they gave "uninvited readings" of their poetry.[61] It was Allen's first visit to Canada—his fourth foreign country. All through their trip, Snyder filled Ginsberg's head with talk of Asia, further fuelling Allen's desire to visit the massive continent.

First, however, he had his eye on Europe, and was planning it out with Orlovsky. The itinerary changed from day to day, but the central problem remained— how would he afford it? Despite being a famous poet (at least in certain circles), he was broke. For years all his letters were filled with ideas of places to visit but he always found that money stood between him and wherever he wanted to go. Once again, he looked to the sea for financial support. He wrote his brother on Boxing Day, 1955, to say that he thought three or four months at sea would be enough to support him for seven or eight months travelling around Europe. He even suggested the possibility of a dream round-the-world trip on a ship, but admitted that the chances were "slight." He began applying for a job in December, but it wasn't until May that he was given a job.

By the end of the month, he was working as a yeo-man-storekeeper on the *U.S.N.S. Pvt. Joseph F. Merrell*, on an annual salary of a little more than $5,000. Of this, he was able to save more than $300 per month towards his next trip. On 9th June, while Ginsberg was on shore, temporarily visiting Berkeley, he received a telegram to say that his mother had suddenly passed away. He did not attend her funeral, and was later tormented by the fact that there were not enough Jewish men in attendance to read a Kaddish, the Jewish funeral rites. Allen swore to write his own Kaddish for his mother, but would not manage to do it satisfactorily for another few years. His fragile emotional state took a further hit when his new ship, the *U.S.N.S. Sgt. Jack J. Pendleton*, stopped in Tacoma on its way to the Arctic Circle. Here, Ginsberg's forwarded mail included a letter from Naomi, written not long before her death.

The ship made stops at Portland and Seattle, and moved back up and down the coast between Washington and California before heading off to supply the Distant Early Warning line radar system that aimed to defend the United States against its new Cold War enemy. On 27th July, they passed through the Bering Strait, a fifty mile stretch of water between the United States and the Soviet Union—his mother's birthplace. Birds flew between the continents, unhindered by the Cold War, language, culture, governments, or anything else that prohibited humans from so readily doing the same thing.

Anchored near Wainwright, Alaska, Ginsberg was

disappointed to see nothing of interest. Although earlier he had been excited by the prospect of "the actual Arctic and glorious North Pole,"[62] he found there were no animals and the land was just a distant blur. The sea was grey and the days lasted all night, which seemed like torture to him. The crew was not allowed off the ship, lest they transmit any diseases to the local indigenous population, and Ginsberg was trapped with his depression, thinking about his lost childhood and his mother. Worse, he was dreaming incestuous dreams about his mother and father, and had frustrating homosexual fantasies about his fellow crew. Here he wrote "Many Loves," a poem lamenting his now decade-long infatuation with Neal Cassady.

But it was not all bad. His work was minimal, allowing him many free hours for reading. He worked his way chronologically through Shakespeare, as well as some "mostly pious works" including the Bible and the Diamond Sutra.[63] He had some proof copies of *Howl and Other Poems* and used the ship's equipment to mimeograph fifty-two copies of "Siesta in Xbalba," which he sent to friends and family. He kept his focus on a trip to Europe, although now he viewed it as a gateway to Russia, where he planned to meet with his family and discover more about his roots. He asked his grandmother to put him in touch with his relatives, and outlined his plans to travel cheaply by rail now that both countries had agreed to allow tourists to move between them. Although since returning from Mexico he had planned various trips—to South America, India, Japan, and elsewhere—this one seemed the most likely to be realised as his mother had unexpectedly left him a thousand dollars in her will. "So I will be rich enough to actually travel and live for several years now," he said.[64]

Mexico Again

Ginsberg arrived back in San Francisco in September, 1956, and had money to burn. Europe was still his primary objective, but as with his trip from New York to California in 1953-54, he was going to take a rather circuitous route. This time he intended to travel to Paris via Mexico City, New York, and Tangier. After giving a joint final poetry reading in San Francisco, Allen and Gregory Corso hitch-hiked from San Francisco to Los Angeles, where they stayed a week before Peter Orlovsky and his brother, Lafcadio, joined them, and together they travelled to Tijuana. They then took a bus to Guadalajara, where they met with the poet Denise Levertov, whose work impressed Allen. They picnicked on the edge of La Barranca Canyon and wandered about the night markets. Then, through a combination of buses and trains, they made it to Mexico City, where they met Kerouac and spent two weeks sightseeing.

For this entire trip, Ginsberg generously bankrolled his friends' activities so that they would be free to "goof" instead of thinking about money. He intended to support all of his friends not only in Mexico but also through their journey into Europe, and believed that Corso's new poem would secure "fellowships and grants and awards" that would also help pay for the

Beat poets to roam freely.[65] Ginsberg wanted to play the role of tourist, which he so often did in his travels, and wandered about with his guidebook in hand, paying no attention to prices. He saw the floating gardens, museums, the Pyramid of the Sun, the ballet, and smoked a lot of marijuana. Peter slept with the local prostitutes and caught gonorrhoea, which he dutifully passed along to Allen, and they all engaged in "big orgies."[66] Orgies had become a rather common pastime for Peter and Allen, and one that they would continue in future travels.

On 1st December, they all—minus Corso, who stayed behind to wait for airfare—drove from Mexico City to New York City on a five-day-long car ride fuelled by Benzedrine and alcohol, all once again paid for by Allen at a cost of $135.

Allen applied for his first passport on 4th January, intending to depart for Tangier with Kerouac later that month, but the trip was delayed. Ginsberg was still expectant that this trip would ultimately lead to a journey through Russia, so he visited the embassy and read some Russian poetry by way of preparation. During this time, he wasn't writing much himself and had more or less gotten into a routine that would dominate his life for the next forty years—being a literary celebrity, albeit at this stage a rather minor one. It seemed he spent all his time trying to get *Howl* reviewed, rather than writing another book. He was looking forward to his trip as it meant "time to go back to solitude again"[67] – a clear nod to his time in Mexico, when he was able to write "Siesta in Xbalba" and develop the voice and perspective needed to make his great poetic breakthrough.

In mid-February, Kerouac departed for Morocco using money he borrowed from Allen, and soon after Corso left for Paris. Allen and Peter were left behind to deal with Orlovsky family problems. When everything was more or less sorted, a tugboat strike further delayed their departure, but eventually they left New York on 10th March, heading for Casablanca on a Yugoslavian freighter called *Hrvatska*.

Tangier

The journey across the Atlantic took nine days, and in Casablanca Ginsberg and Orlovsky spent two days looking around before taking a boat north to Tangier. Due to its location at the meeting of the Atlantic Ocean and Mediterranean Sea, Tangier had been a city of great importance for many civilisations throughout history, and between 1924 and 1956 it had functioned as an "international zone," jointly administered by Belgium, France, Britain, Italy, the Netherlands, Portugal, and Spain. However, nine months prior to Ginsberg's arrival, it had been integrated with the rest of Morocco. Bizarrely, although Tangier is clearly located on the African continent, Ginsberg refers to it throughout his entire correspondence from the period as part of Europe.

It had been William S. Burroughs who had convinced Allen to visit Tangier, comparing it to Mexico but claiming it was far safer. Burroughs had chosen it after reading Paul Bowles' *The Sheltering Sky* and *Let it Come Down*, deciding that Tangier's famously permissive attitudes were conducive to his own outlaw lifestyle. He had felt smothered in the United States, so he had moved to Texas, which he considered the last frontier, before going further south to Mexico and South America, where he was comparatively free. But he had never been happy for very long in any of these places. He sought somewhere where he could procure drugs and gay sex without being hassled by the authorities, as well as somewhere he could easily survive on the allowance he received from his family. Tangier in the fifties was a magnet for gay tourists because of its tolerance of homosexuality, and a huge gulf in wealth between locals and expats meant there was always a thriving trade in prostitution. Burroughs never dealt well with authority, and in Tangier he found he could be free, particularly at a hotel called Villa el-Muniria, where the landlady was a former brothel-owner. Burroughs, who had wanted to be a spy or a detective as a young man, was also more than likely drawn by the city's legendary status as a hotbed of international espionage. In any case, he was content in Tangier for a while, and it served as his home for four years as he wrote a vast manuscript that would one day become his most famous novel, *Naked Lunch*.

Kerouac had arrived about a month before Ginsberg and Orlovsky, but, as Allen later reflected, "Jack was no good out of America."[68] Kerouac was a very different type of traveller from Allen, and complained bitterly about everything, quickly growing homesick. After exploring the Medina in Casablanca, Allen and Peter arrived in Tangier to find Jack and Bill waiting for them at the harbour, but the big Beat reunion didn't last long. Kerouac took off the next day for his own tour of Europe. He later wrote Allen with lots of advice about travelling France and England, in particular recommending that Allen make the most of his time in Paris. "You will love it," he told his friend.[69]

Fortunately for Burroughs, Ginsberg was happy to pick up where Kerouac left off and helped him organise his manuscript, typing and structuring the vast collection of pages, and extracting fragments from letters he'd sent Allen during his South American travels. Although Allen was eager to get out and see the sights— being the insatiable tourist that he was—he spent five or six hours each day just working on Burroughs' book. At night Ginsberg and Burroughs stayed up late, talking about art and smoking marijuana. There was plenty of cheap opium, too. Paul Bowles stopped by often, and the painter Francis Bacon, whose work Allen had seen in New York and San Francisco, was soon part of their group. The two men told Allen about India and Kenya, countries he'd soon see for himself. There was a garden filled with roses and cats, and a rooftop patio overlooking the perfect green sea. In the afternoons he sat in the Arab quarter drinking mint tea while reading the Koran and Herman Melville, and as the sun fell over the Atlantic Ocean, they cooked great meals and smoked fat joints. On a clear day, standing in the right place, you could see across the water to Gibraltar and Spain, and it was just possible to make out the ancient structures that called out to Allen from classical Europe.

After a week, Ginsberg had decided he would stay in Tangier for a long time, partly because he liked it there and partly because he just didn't have the funds to move on. The money he'd earned and inherited had been squandered on his excursion to Mexico, a loan to Kerouac, and the boat ride to Africa. Peter's disability cheque had been increased from $17.50 to $50 per month on account of his obvious mental problems, and William Carlos Williams had helped Allen get a $200 poetry grant, but nonetheless they were flat broke in Tangier. For the time being, he was dependent upon Burroughs, and in addition to helping him with *Naked Lunch*, Allen also did most of the housework to earn his keep.

Perhaps it was predictable that after two months of this situation, Ginsberg and Orlovsky both grew weary. Allen told Gary Snyder that he was "Burroughs' slave" in Tangier and that it had been an "awful routine."[70]* Despite the seemingly conducive atmosphere, he hadn't actually written any poetry, partly due to reservations he had over "Howl." Moreover, Burroughs didn't care for Orlovsky, and teased him cruelly. It wasn't long before they were planning an escape—the journey through Europe that Ginsberg had long desired. Both Ginsberg and Orlovsky were desperate to leave, but it seemed that whenever they attempted to do so, they became ill and had to postpone. Allen had a guidebook for Spain, which he perused, and mapped out a journey

---

* "routine" here has a double meaning, as Burroughs' own twisted fantasies (such as those that made up Naked Lunch) were called routines.

that would allow him to see the great achievements of European history, with a particular emphasis on art—stopping off at the finest galleries and the locations where the great painters did their best work. He aimed to travel cheaply up through Spain, across Southern France, and through Italy to Venice, where they could stay with Alan Ansen, whom Allen had met in New York years earlier. Ansen had also helped work on *Naked Lunch* together with Allen in Tangier. They had almost no money, but a lot of faith: "guess things will work out alright, whatever happens."[71]

Allen's First Tour of Europe

For years, Ginsberg had dreamed of travelling Europe. Much of his reading as a young man had been from the great British and French writers, and he was fond of the great artists of Holland, Spain, and Germany. In Mexico, his yearning to live in the Old World had reached a fever pitch:

> . . . I must as soon as possible go to live awhile in Europe—think of the marvellous facades and palaces of dank Venice alone for instance, which will be digged in spacious St. Mark's Square dusk by us among pigeons of Europe and Eyetalian [Italian] beggars as some slow silent stage presentation of melancholy cloaked Byronic traveler passing thru in sad ballet.

To say nothing of hollow old Catholic Rome. Prague! the very name conjures a mirage of centuries, the Golem, ghettoes, stone kinds and fountains of dark lions and grey cherubs, students drinking beer and duelling thru the night. And perhaps sweet Moscow. Then there is Paris. Paris! City of Light! *ici mouru* Racine! Here Proust sipped his delicate tea, here Jean Gabin stared out over the roofs with his mistress crying in bed, glum. Memories, ancient waltzes, *tristesse de la lune*, all the tenderness of antiquity and the angel gentility of civilization, with the Eiffel tower and strange city mystics *a la* Cocteau and Rimbaud and most of the tearful reality of the old world places. Even wish to see Londres, London of great bells and banking houses old as time, where liveth still in silence Seymour [Wyes] waiting for a winking eye from us undoubtedly.[72]

On 11th June, 1957, with just $150 in their pockets, Ginsberg and Orlovsky took a ferry from Tangiers to Algeciras, a little west of Gibraltar. On the two-hour boat ride they saw dolphins jumping out of the water ahead of them, which Ginsberg took as a rather good omen. Indeed, they found Algeciras even cheaper than Tangier, and enjoyed their first taste of European café culture. They spent $15 on rail passes that allowed them reduced fares around the country, and waited in a long line by the docks to board a train to Granada because Allen had "read about it in grammar school."[73] The train chugged through Andalucía "through Lorca sunset thru mountains and red sunset between castle hills without dragons" to Granada, where Allen saw Alhambra—a Moorish relic that is part fort, part palace—as Peter slept.[74] Allen claimed to get high from examining the intricate Arabic designs, although he was also carrying a small amount of marijuana from Tangier that no doubt contributed. They also took in the city's big cathedral and searched its giant interior for an image of St. Francis painted by El Greco, and at night Allen wandered the streets and listened to gypsies singing and dancing to Flamenco music.

Next, they took a train to Seville to see the Cathedral de Sevilla, and spent two nights there wandering the streets with high walls and awnings to keep the sun off, before moving on to Córdoba to see the Great Mosque and the Roman bridge over Guadalquivir River, which Allen called "very ancient and timeless."[75] He spent two hours sitting by the river watching women wash clothes, and was transported back through the millennia in his mind, thinking of all the people who'd crossed the bridge. From Córdoba they took an all-night train north to the capital city, Madrid, arriving on 21st June. Naturally, he made a bee-line for Museo del Prado, one of the finest art collections in the world, and certainly the best in Spain. Viewing the great paintings of Europe had been one of the prime motivations in visiting the continent, and the Prado did not disappoint. Here he viewed works by Breughel, Bosch,

El Greco, Goya, Velasquez, and Rubens. "We got a good education now," he told Kerouac.[76] He spent hours viewing individual paintings, and decided that Fra Angelico's *The Anunciación* was the greatest painting of all time. In a long Kerouacian letter he wrote to Kerouac, he described the picture vividly. This is just a very short excerpt of that description:

> . . . a huge picture made out of clearest pearly ivory white and shining green and delicious red full of delicate hand touches of long gowns and lines and kneeling angels and rosy virgin cool, and god's gold small hands ushering out radiances of long golden streams of light from the upper left corner, thru which rides a dove with a halo down to the virgin kneeling and bowing down with her robes settling round her like in a dream underwater. . .[77]

Art had been a great motivating force in bringing Allen to Europe and the Prado was his first major gallery. Yet it was not his last. He returned the next day and the day after that, this time high on marijuana, and continued to visit all the museums and galleries he could on this tour and others. The places he visited on this trip were determined to a great extent by what famous paintings he could view. He returned to Europe many times over the course of his life and visited just about every major art collection available to him. Bill Morgan referred to it as "museum fever."[78] Ginsberg himself told Kerouac:

> At that instant I got Europe hungry and museum hungry and realised all the treasures of Europe all over, in Italy & Spain & Moscow & Paris, all the vast collections of infinite pictures.[79]

In Madrid, Orlovsky was sick with food poisoning and Allen spent much of his time exploring the city alone, including his long solo visits to the Prado. When Peter got better, they took in a bullfight and then made a daytrip to Toledo, seventy kilometres south. They spent a day hiking around looking for the view that inspired El Greco's painting, *View of Toledo*, but couldn't find it. Food here was cheap, although the hotel was more expensive than they'd have liked. Overall, they enjoyed Madrid and looked into the possibility of staying long-term, but after a few days of searching for jobs it looked unlikely they'd find anything, and so they continued north towards France.

Next was Barcelona, where they visited the Barrio Chino in pursuit of the scene portrayed by Jean Genet in his novels, but failed to find the same wild atmosphere of "beggars, thieves, fairies and whores."[80] Instead, they visited more museums and then saw Antoni Gaudí's La Sagrada Família, whose construction had begun in 1885 and continued then, in 1957. (Note: It continues still fifty-two years later in 2019.) Allen was stunned, comparing it rather oddly to both a gingerbread castle and the Kremlin. They also saw another

Gaudí project, Park Güell, and took the funicular up Mount Tibidabo, where they had incredible views of the city. In his travels, Ginsberg often made odd associations between places, and Barcelona somehow reminded him of Harlem. They continued to eat cheaply and see whatever paintings were on offer, before taking off for the border with France.

They took the train north and crossed into France, again loaded down with marijuana, heading for the town of Perpignan. Ginsberg had learned from another poet that Perpignan was a centre of fruit production and thus sent countless trucks all over the country, thereby making it the ideal place from which to hitchhike. However, they had arrived very late and found the town completely empty, so they had to sleep outdoors under a tree. At 5am the trucks began to roll through town, but none would pick them up. All the cars were small by American standards, and would never accommodate two extra travellers with backpacks. Ginsberg should have known this, as Kerouac had warned him in a letter that there was "no good hitching in Europe," referring in particular to France.[81]

When they finally did get picked up, after walking several miles, the car took them only ten kilometres and they were soon stuck in another hopeless little town. By the end of the day, though, someone had taken pity on them and drove them as far as Beziere. Ginsberg, with his astounding memory for all things poetic, recalled Ezra Pound describing this little place as a hub of poetic activity. Alas, they found little of interest except a funeral and a church, and after many more hours of failed hitch-hiking they gave up and boarded a train to Montpellier. By now their wallets were virtually empty and they were desperate to get to Venice, where they could live for free until they found the cash to move on.

In Montpellier, they happened upon a Communist cell meeting in a bookstore and proceeded to get into an argument with the group's leader about politics and philosophy. Ginsberg was appalled by their ideas but delighted that in France, unlike America, people were free to assemble regardless of their political views. It made him think of how America had lost its way. They had very little time in Montpellier because of their financial situation, and ran around trying to see everything before their train to Marseille. While walking around the old town they spotted an odd-looking man with a black beard whom they had seen in Barcelona, and the three of them sat on a bench, holding hands and trying to communicate despite having no common language. Still, it seemed to Allen that they transcended verbal communication and spoke through their hearts. The man was from Austria and had walked across Europe all by himself, heaving a giant backpack. Allen was very impressed, and their brief encounter left a deep impression on him. "That's how we should all love each other," he said, explaining how the man had given him and Peter a bunch of grains for their train ride.[82]

They rode the train along the "Cézanne coast" to Marseille, and from there they crossed the border into Italy. They spent one day and one night in Milan before heading east to Venice, arriving on 1st July. In Venice they were free to stay indefinitely, without worrying too much about money. They lived happily with Alan Ansen on the Calle della Carrozze, and as he had done with Burroughs in Tangier, Ginsberg paid his way by doing the chores. They also had $50 a month coming in from Orlovsky's disability allowance. From his window, Allen could see the Grand Canal, and each day he set out in his role as indefatigable tourist to see all the sights his guidebooks recommended, including all of the museums in town. Of course, he visited the Piazza San Marco and the great cathedral, outside of which there were cafés and music and dancing, and inside the ornate building had floors that rippled where the building sank into the mud beneath it. Although he had enjoyed Spain, his trip thus far had been very rushed. In Venice, however, he found what he was looking for. Barry Miles notes in his Ginsberg biography:

> This was the Old World of Europe that Ginsberg dreamed of in Chiapas and California, and he was utterly enthralled.[83]

Although broke, on 27th July they managed a "wild trip" to Florence, Rome, and Assisi.[84] In Florence, Ginsberg spent a day and a half at the Uffizi gallery, another of Europe's great art collections. As he had done in Mexico, Allen somehow managed to acquire a student card and got into the gallery for free. There were works by Botticelli, da Vinci, Giotto, Rembrandt, and other masters. Many of these included visions that entranced Ginsberg. He saw Michelangelo's David and some of his other sculptures, as well as more by Fra Angelico, whose painting had captivated him in Madrid. Even outside the museums the streets seemed filled with art. In particular, they enjoyed viewing statues of nude men that helped fuel a growing anti-Catholic sentiment within the poet.

At this time, back in the U.S., Lawrence Ferlinghetti's City Lights was going up against the government in a famous obscenity trial over Ginsberg's *Howl and Other Poems*. Allen was in contact with Ferlinghetti and others about the trial but did not return to the U.S. during the process. During the summer of the trial, Ginsberg commented often in his letters about nude paintings and statues, and it is likely he was impressed by the freedom of expression. He told his father that the fact David was naked was Michelangelo's "great historical statement," no doubt thinking of his own historical statement, "Howl," whose fate presently hung in the balance. [85]

After three days in Florence they took a train to Rome and stayed in a student dormitory whilst exploring the city by foot. They visited the Coliseum, St. Peter's Basilica, the Forum, Palatine Hills, Trevi Fountain, and the Protestant Cemetery, where John Keats and Percy Bysshe Shelley were buried. Allen picked two clovers from Shelley's grave—one to send to Corso, and one to his father, Louis. They spent an afternoon exploring the ruins and the beach at Ostia, and then got high at the Vatican. After seeing the wondrous naked statues and paintings of Italy and Spain, Allen was appalled that the church had painted over Michelangelo's *Last Judgment* in order to hide the nudity, and had added fig leaves to the otherwise nude statues. "I almost flipped," he said of seeing the fig leaves.[86]

Despite his feelings towards censorship of his own work and that of the Renaissance masters, and despite being almost penniless, Allen was feeling happy and adventurous, and the two men took off on a train for Assisi, birthplace of St. Francis, located in the beautiful Umbrian Valley. They arrived looking more than a little dishevelled, not unlike St. Francis himself:

> . . . we came into town unshaven & dirty & eating milk & salami & fruit on the way, invaded the Franciscan monastery, met all the English speaking monks & argued about St. Francis & looked at his tomb & relics & robes & climbed up hills to see caves where he'd hidden & secret hermitages he'd spent winters in, all in hot summer sun, with small bagful of food & rundown heels & needing a haircut & a broken straw hat . . .[87]

They begged for assistance but were turned down by the monks and ended up rolling out their sleeping bags on the monastery lawn, fellating each other in the moonlight in front of the church doors. The next day, Ginsberg continued to bug the monks, poking holes in their myths, complaining about the fig leaves, and reading them his poems (which he thought was a very Franciscan thing to do). By the time they left, the monks were thoroughly annoyed with Ginsberg, and

Ginsberg was equally disgusted by the Catholic Church: a "vast nasty thought control organisation."[88] The monks, he thought, were "nothing but a bunch of hard up, fig-leaving, psychotic politicians."[89]

Still, once again, despite everything, he was elated. "This is about the best & funniest time I've had since been in Europe."[90] They decided to hitch-hike back to Venice via Florence, where they returned once again to the Uffizi and the Piazza della Signoria, and Perugia, where Allen continued to indulge his "museum fever." On the way, they slept in fields during the pleasant summer nights and found that food was so cheap they could afford to eat well even on their meagre budget. They hopped a train for part of the way, hiding from the conductor in the toilet, and arrived back in Venice with absolutely no money in their pockets. Thankfully, when they arrived in Venice, they found a royalty cheque and Peter's disability cheque waiting for them.

They had their eyes set on Paris, but for the time being it just wasn't financially feasible, so they stayed with Ansen a little longer. Ginsberg was starting to write again, although he noted that nothing of any real significance was produced, and he was encouraging Ansen to get into writing, too. During this time, he was reading Whitman's *Democratic Vistas*, which was highly influential on his political and social views. To Ginsberg, it seemed Whitman agreed with Spengler about the fall of western civilisation—"he says if we don't produce bards and spiritual America and if materialism greed takes over we be 'the fabled damned among nations'".[91]

When *Time* magazine called from Rome, asking him for an interview about the on-going "Howl" trial, he suggested they pay him to visit Rome, and so he made another trip to the capital on 22nd August. *Time* agreed to pay his airfare and give him $35 for two days' expenses, which he used to travel Italy for a nearly a fortnight—this time on his own, having left Peter in Venice. He further explored Rome and the surrounding areas, watched the Pope say Mass, got drunk, and then took a train to Naples to see a more authentic slice of Italian life. Once again, he visited all the museums and art galleries on offer, including the pornographic works of Pompeii, and then climbed to the top of Mount Vesuvius. After sliding down the side of the steaming volcano, he explored the ruins of Pompeii, delighted to find nude statues still surviving, as well as crude graffiti in an ancient brothel. The land here was covered in vineyards, and Allen stopped off along the way to pilfer big blue grapes as he traipsed across the landscape.

After visiting nearby Capri and returning to Naples to see the ruins of Cuma, Ginsberg then sailed to the Isle of Ischia, where he knew W.H. Auden spent his summers. Allen found him drinking at an establishment called Marie's Bar with friends (a group of "dull chatty literary old fairies"[92]) one evening and intruded upon their conversation, arguing angrily with them about Walt Whitman. Ginsberg was appalled by Auden's overly-rationalistic way of discussing literature, saying he "argued only lunacy"[93] and ended up leaving the bar drunk, calling the group "a bunch of shits."[94]

Although Auden was a disappointment, Ginsberg

very much enjoyed Ischia. He found it to be a peaceful place to spend a few days swimming and exploring, and much less touristy than Capri. He climbed the big mountain, Epomeo, in the middle of the island, and walked all over, taking in the cliffs and jutting peninsulas. However, he had little time to spend there, and travelled quickly to Venice by boat, train, and airplane, ready to plan the next big adventure.

The Beat Hotel

After receiving a hundred dollar cheque from City Lights for *Howl and Other Poems* and fifty from his brother Eugene, Allen and Peter were finally able to take off towards Paris in September. In order to make the most of their trip, they travelled through Austria and Germany, stopping off in Vienna to view yet more paintings by Brueghel and see an opera. They tried to watch Mozart's Don Juan but were kicked out in the middle. Next, they saw Germany and spent four days exploring Munich and the Dachau concentration camp. They stayed with one of Allen's friends, who kindly showed them around the city, taking them to beer gardens and jazz bars. Allen called the trip "a confused vision of Hitlerian Art museums."[95]

In Venice, Ansen had introduced Ginsberg and Orlovsky to a Dutch artist called Guy Harloff, who lived in a small hotel in the Latin Quarter of Paris. It was located at 9 rue Git-le-Couer, and functioned as a sort of artists' colony. The place was always full because it was cheap and the landlady, Madame Rachou, was incredibly permissive by the standards of the day. She had run the hotel since 1933 and was fond of the company of artists, even allowing them to sometimes pay in artwork rather than cash. The hotel was class-13, meaning it only had to meet the most basic of standards, and even then Madame Rachou's good relationship with the police meant that these were seldom met. Sheets were rarely changed, electricity would frequently go out, and for a toilet there was simply a hole in the ground and newspaper hanging in lieu of toilet paper.[96] Although terribly basic, the bohemian environment (which included not just the hotel but the surrounding streets) ensured that the hotel attracted a certain type of resident, and it soon became known as "The Beat Hotel."

When they arrived in Paris, Ginsberg was immediately impressed:

> Paris is beautiful—the only city I've seen so far that would tempt me to expatriate & settle down. The rest of Europe has been interesting, and each city has its one, two or three marvels or charms, but Paris has universal interest and permanent charm as a living place. I'll try to stay here for a half a year and then come home, unless I get enough money for trip to the Far East . . . Best place in Europe so far.[97]

However, as lovely as Paris proved to be, when Allen and Peter arrived, they found that there were no rooms available at the Beat Hotel until 15th October, several weeks away, and that Gregory Corso, whom they had intended to visit, had just left for Amsterdam. They took in the sights for a week, but struggled to keep under budget. Everywhere else was expensive and with no room they had nowhere to cook. They stayed in a hotel by the Seine and spent a few days sleeping at Le Mistral, a bookstore run by a friend of Ferlinghetti called George Whitman, before taking off for Amsterdam to see Corso and wait for a room to be vacated at the Beat Hotel. In a flurry of letters during mid-September, Corso told Allen that Amsterdam was the "most beautiful city I have ever seen" and vividly described a wild literary scene where everyone spoke and published in English, and people were reprinting and reviewing *Howl*. He told Allen that he'd been distributing copies of *Howl* throughout the city, essentially making Allen into a celebrity, as well as rubbing shoulders with other "famous writers."[98]

Amsterdam, they found, was a wonderful city. Sleeping on Corso's floor, they were able to take in the calm canal scene by day and the wild hipster bars at night. This was a city where people appreciated good literature, Ginsberg thought. There were literary journals, poetry bars, and people were passionate about different literary movements. He and Corso wrote an article about the Beat Generation for a magazine and earned enough cash to survive there for three weeks. Prostitution was legal, which pleased Peter, and Allen felt that Holland—like much of Europe—was far more advanced in its racial relations than the U.S., where the Little Rock Crisis was going on. There were art galleries brimming with paintings by Van Gogh, Vermeer, and Rembrandt, and they found cheap Indonesian food to sustain them as they explored this fascinating city. It had been flattened during the Second World War, and Allen observed that after having been rebuilt, it wasn't just modern, it was "futuristic."[99] From the window of a train, on one of his trips through Holland, he could see "low green fields & canals & windmills & cows—long plain, huge sky, everything still & green, except for windmill turning furiously in the unseen wind."[100] They saw the museums of Rotterdam, hitch-hiked across the border into Belgium, and even contemplated going north to Sweden, but soon it was time to get back to France.

On 15th October, the three men returned to Paris to take up residence at the Beat Hotel, where Ginsberg would stay for the next ten months. Rooms cost about thirty dollars per month, and were filled with all manner of unusual people. The first room Allen and Peter were given was particularly unpleasant, and a little more expensive than the others, but after a week they were moved to the third floor, which was far more comfortable and cost less than the first. This room had gas for Allen to cook with, and he remarked in a letter to his father that it didn't matter how little cash he had in his pocket, for he would always be able to "live comfortably" if he had the facilities to cook. Corso stayed with them for a while, three men in a small bed, until he was able to take his own room. Allen unpacked his typewriter and prepared himself for a literary outpouring. Over the previous six months he had seen a great deal, but done very little writing except for letters. "Correspondence mounts & is being bad problem now," he had written his father from Venice.[101]

Back in 1952, mired in self-doubt, Allen had contemplated a trip to Paris, but rejected what he considered the hackneyed story of a young American writer going there to work on his art. This was the Beat Generation, not the Lost Generation. "It's such egotism to be a lonely writer in Europe," he had once told Kerouac.[102] Yet five years later, this great literary city was where Ginsberg began work on his next great poem. In the U.S. he was now famous as the author of "Howl," which was selling well and causing a storm in the American media, but Allen was keen to move on to the next work, and Paris would prove fertile ground for him during his stay. In between trips to the Louvre and Notre Dame, subterranean exploration in the catacombs, and walks along the Seine and around the Eiffel Tower, he took pleasure in the city's café culture, which provided both inspiration and location for his writing. He was also keenly aware that these places were where some of the world's greatest writers and artists had sat and nursed coffees while talking over the issues of their day, and when he went out he saw all the "literary and theatrical types" of *his* day were still there.[103]

In early November, at Le Select on Blvd Montparnasse, which was his favourite out of the numerous cafés he visited, he began work on a poem that many consider to be his greatest, "Kaddish."* He had, of course, been planning to write an elegy for his mother since her death more than a year earlier; however, it was France that inspired him to action. In Paris, he had written poems about Naomi, but these never made it into "Kaddish." Some utilised very long lines and others very short. However, the section that he wrote at Le Select was used more or less unchanged in Part IV of "Kaddish,"and was very much a product of his time in France. In Paris, Ginsberg had been improving his French skills and wrote Kerouac that after a few weeks in France he was able to read poetry—but not full novels—in French. A young friend called Jean-Jacque Lebel had introduced him to the work of André Breton, and it is clear from the lines Ginsberg wrote at Le Select that he had read Breton's "L'Union Libre" ("Free Union") and was influenced by its structure.

The lines he wrote at Le Select were about his mother, but they also touched upon another subject that was starting to dominate Allen's thoughts. When he wrote "with your eyes of America taking a Fall" he was returning to an idea that first interested him during his time at Columbia. Bill Morgan expanded upon this idea in his biography:

> Through his travels Allen was learning
> that the United States had been actively

---

* The Café Select is where Hart Crane once got drunk and was beaten severely by police officers. Ginsberg was more than likely aware of this fact.

supporting too many dictators, and he feared that all America's past mistakes would come home to roost. The decline of America was coming earlier than anyone had predicted, and he prophesied that Spengler's ideas would soon come to fruition, just as he, Burroughs, and Kerouac had agreed more than ten years earlier.[104]

Of course, Ginsberg had never been the flag-waving patriot type, but his time outside the United States was increasingly affecting his world view, and in France he continued a process of politicisation that had really started in Mexico, and which would continue over the coming years until he emerged as an anti-war icon in the sixties. Michael Schumacher said that, "for the first time in his life, Allen was seeing the United States through the eyes of others. In talking to Europeans, and reading their newspapers and magazines, Allen felt the stripping away of any Americentricity he might have possessed."[105] In Paris, he began work on a "monstrous and golden political or historical poem about the fall of America"* called "Death to Van Gogh's Ear," written in December, 1957:

> the government of America also will fall but how
> can America fall

---

* The term "fall of America," which he used in other letters during this period, would be repeated a decade later as the title of one of his major poetry collections.

> I doubt if anyone will ever fall anymore except
> governments
> fortunately all the governments will fall[106]

The poem discusses the inevitable rise of Asia, which Ginsberg often thought about, and the consequences of the fall of western civilisation. He went on about these concepts in his letters to Kerouac, mentioning in particular the rise of China and the need for America to change its ways or else face ruin. He perhaps jokingly suggested America take a vow of poverty for the sake of spiritual purity, and that he "must call for Holy America make it on beat angel soul . . . otherwise maybe paranoia machine sink down on us from new Asia."[107] To his father, he wrote that America's decline was "inevitable" from his perspective in Europe due to "too much materialistic self indulgence."[108]

On 19th December, President Eisenhower visited Paris for a NATO meeting. Tensions between the United States and the Soviet Union were high, and the sputnik launches had helped confirm Allen's notion of the fall of America. In a letter to Jack Kerouac, he wrote, "Now the bitter American reality encounters the Oriental century to come."[109] Eisenhower's visit made Ginsberg eager once again to visit his mother's homeland, and he began planning for a trip to Moscow. On the same day Eisenhower arrived in Paris, Ginsberg made another literary pilgrimage of sorts, this time to Père Lachaise cemetery, where he stopped by Guillaume Apollinaire's grave and left a copy of *Howl and Other Poems* on the headstone. Here he wrote one of his finest poems, "At

Apollinaire's Grave," which mused on the subjects of mortality, the decline of the West, and literary heritage.

Money continued to be an issue for Ginsberg in Paris, where for periods of time he was very nearly starving at the Beat Hotel. For a year he had tried to live on the royalties generated from his poetry, but even though he was making a lot of sales, the money was pitiful, and Allen was in debt to the local grocer for milk and eggs. When Orlovsky left Paris and headed back to the United States in January, 1958, Allen was left without the V.A. cheque that had more or less sustained them through much of their travels. Fortunately, Kerouac begrudgingly repaid an old debt of $225, allowing Allen to survive in Europe a bit longer.

At the end of 1957 he had been visited by Thomas Parkinson, his old professor from Berkeley, who invited Allen to England. Parkinson now worked with the BBC and was producing programmes that featured recordings of poets, and naturally he thought Allen might want to be included. On 1st February, having been finally repaid by Kerouac, Ginsberg took the train to Calais and then crossed the Channel to England, "the land of Blake," the next day. At this time, London was the biggest city on earth, yet still very much recovering from the Second World War. The old London Allen imagined had been destroyed by German bombs and English land developers. After touring the National Gallery to take in yet more Rembrandts and Vermeers, as well as gaining an appreciation for William Turner ("the only British painter and great genius like Van Gogh"[110]), he met up with Parkinson to record a five minute poetry reading. However, he was quickly stopped by the director, Donald Carne-Ross, who asked Allen to do a full recording of both "Howl" and "A Supermarket in California." Delighted, Allen obliged and gave a fantastic, emotional reading of both poems.

Although he felt lonely in London, Allen managed to meet many new people and make close friends, whom he would see time and again in the future. One poet he met up with was Gael Turnbull, who drove Allen to Stratford-upon-Avon to visit Shakespeare's grave and to Salisbury to see Stonehenge and the cathedral. Next, he visited Oxford and delivered a reading to a group of ecstatic students, performing not only his own work but that of Burroughs, Robert Creeley, Philip Whalen, and Denise Levertov. In London, he read translations of speeches by Khrushchev and Mao Zedong, his views on international politics changing and evolving by the day. His interest in the road east was growing and growing.

After two or three weeks he was back in Paris with Corso and Burroughs, who had also moved in to the burgeoning Beat colony. Ginsberg had been offered a reading at Frankfurt University and was also interested in getting to Berlin to see the "East-West culture-conflict"[111]* but he wanted Burroughs to go with him and Burroughs refused. Soon, though, Allen and Gregory were offered more readings in Oxford by an Indian poet Allen had met there. They quickly headed back to England, where Ginsberg showed Corso around. Again, Allen continued meeting new poets and felt himself

* Berlin was at this point divided but the Wall had not yet been built.

getting closer to literary London. He felt he saw more of England than before, and this time met a wider range of people: "met all the teddy boys and bebop hoodlums & angels around Soho."[112] In Oxford, they harangued W.H. Auden and Dame Edith Sitwell, and at their reading Corso was lambasted by the local student poets, who evidently didn't understand his poem, "Bomb," and pelted him with shoes. They ended up stuck in England for several weeks without any money before escaping back to Paris.

Although Allen had initially enjoyed France, life was becoming more difficult. The Algerian War had caused riots and demonstrations in the capital, and the police responded by becoming oppressive. One day he imagined he saw his mother in a "vast mob rally against DeGaulle."[113] He felt a mixture of homesickness and yet further wanderlust, flitting back and forth between the idea of returning to the United States and going somewhere else. He missed Peter and his family, and talked of finding work on a ship once again in order to raise the money to go home. Yet he was also in some ways afraid of going back to America to "face all them aroused evil forces."[114] He told Gary Snyder that he was now making enough money to consider travelling further afield, and in his letters he mentions plans to see Berlin, Warsaw, and Moscow, as well as Greece and nearby countries, and he even had plans to head to Asia to explore India. He was still eager to see behind the Iron Curtain and sent letters and books to various people there to test the waters, finally deciding that Warsaw was "the most jumping city in Europe now."[115]

Ultimately, he decided to return to the U.S. first and put India top of his list of countries to visit next as in his last months in Paris he and Burroughs had become friends with an eccentric millionaire called Jacques Stern, who convinced Allen that India was the place to visit. Allen decided that he wanted to travel to Calcutta with a few friends, including Stern, to "study Yoga and meet the Sages of India at last."[116]

During his final days in Paris, Allen rubbed shoulders with famous artists like Man Ray, Tristan Tzara, and Marcel Duchamp, and completed his sight-seeing experience with trips to Versailles and Chartres. Then, on 17th July, he set sail for the United States. He'd been gone more than sixteen months by the time he arrived back in New York on 23rd July, passing through the harbour under the Statue of Liberty—the true immigrant experience.

> Skyline is stunning in the mist, when I came in—like all the spires and archi-tecture and cathedrals of Europe all put together on one shelf and more massive height—you get a sense of eternity looking at Manhattan from a boat arriving—the buildings look as if they were manufactur-ing cosmic jazz.[117]

His journey through North Africa and Europe had been transformative. Not only had he seen "a lot of classical Europe [and] got all hung up on painting for the first time,"[118] but he had developed his poetic technique further and become more engaged with political thought. Even by March, his letters to Louis highlight an awareness of his own political views being impossible to have developed at home in the U.S., as he said, "I had in US always taken it for granted that the US could really basically do no wrong."[119] Now, however, he was painfully aware of the problems in the world and America's role in creating or sustaining them. At the Beat Hotel, he had also begun to develop notions of "Love bliss" which would develop into the "Free Love" that pervaded the hippie scene in the sixties. He could speak French, had made countless new contacts across the continent, and had a headful of imagery that would make appearances in his poetry for the rest of his life. In addition, he was now a veteran traveller. Though it was Kerouac who became famous for his exploits on the road, it was Ginsberg who had by now visited fourteen countries and could survive seemingly anywhere for long periods of time, making valuable friends and contacts everywhere he went regardless of language, immersing himself in the culture, and soaking up the history. Even a perpetual lack of funds couldn't stop him. Allen had gone out into the world with little money in his pocket and survived once again on his wits and abilities as a poet, with a few charitable donations from friends and family along the way. Every time he managed to get some more money he had used it to extend his travels and have new experiences, and each of these shaped his outlook and his poetry in some way.

South America

Back in the United States, Ginsberg embarked upon a reading tour. Previously, he had been conflicted about reading poetry for money, but for a number of reasons he had finally come to conclude that it was something he ought to do, and it dominated his life for the next forty years. He was now the *de facto* Beat Generation spokesperson, with Kerouac becoming increasingly reclusive and Burroughs and Corso remaining in Paris. In addition to his readings, he continued to promote Beat literature and push for causes like marijuana legalisation.

One weekend in November, when he finally found the time, he sat down and wrote from six o'clock on Saturday morning to ten o'clock on Sunday evening, fuelled by morphine, Methedrine, and Dexadrine, and sustained by coffee and eggs that Peter brought quietly into his room. The result was parts one and two of "Kaddish," which he had begun in Paris. The Parisian section became part four, and a third was added to link it with the second. Whereas in previous works he had sought to capture the American voice, in "Kaddish" he was more interested in pursuing a vocal expression of emotion based in suffering—a universal voice forged from his own explorations of the world beyond America's shores. It was a poem about a woman born in Russia, set in America, whose construction began in France, and whose voice was a product of Allen's experiences in Mexico, Morocco, and elsewhere. On his journeys he often felt guilty for not writing enough poetry, but as he explained to Robert LaVigne, using "Kaddish" as an example, when he was out in the world not writing, he was gathering the material and inspiration required to create art—and "Kaddish," he believed, was his finest creation.[120]

During 1959, Ginsberg travelled frequently across America, giving readings in different cities. On one such trip, he had his first journey on a jet plane, which he enjoyed, saying it was "like a movie of Topographical Geography."[121] He soon grew tired of the travel involved, yet yearned for his own free travels. Already he missed "the joy of lone travelling,"[122] and recorded in his journal dreams of seeing Europe once again. He also wished to travel across the United States, although not like his mad dash over the continent with Neal Cassady, or like the hurried flights he took from poetry reading to poetry reading. This time he wanted to take in the real America. In the summer, after receiving a large check for an article he wrote together with Jack Kerouac, he drove from California to New Jersey with Orlovsky and Robert Creeley, stopping off to see the Grand Canyon, Mount Rushmore, the Black Hills, and the Walt Whitman House in Camden, New Jersey. He had travelled America before, but now he was able to be a proper tourist.

In November, Allen was invited by Fernando Alegria to a poetry conference in South America. After only a year and a half back in the U.S., he viewed it as a welcome escape from his now hectic life of poetry readings and dealing with publishers on behalf of his friends. "I'm dragged and depressed by literary politics," he wrote

Kerouac, who replied by telling his friend to get out and see the world some more or else waste his life sitting at home.[123] He wanted Orlovsky to join him, but Peter's passport had been seized after coming back from Paris on a government loan, and anyway, it was unlikely the conference organisers would have paid his fare. They had agreed to purchase for Allen an open-ended roundtrip ticket to Chile mostly because one of them had illegally published "Howl" and felt guilty. In any case, the ticket allowed for short journeys within South America, and so Allen decided to take advantage by staying in South America for about two months, which he later extended to six.

On 14th January, 1960, he flew from Newark to Santiago with Lawrence Ferlinghetti, sitting part of the way in the cockpit, talking to the pilots and looking out over the Andes. It was a twenty-four-hour flight from a bitterly cold winter in New York to a sweltering Chilean summer. Looking down at the Andes, he compared what he saw to the landscape of California. During the flight, he prepared for his time in South America by reading the work of renowned Chilean poet, Pablo Neruda.

The poetry conference lasted just one week, but he found it a little boring, calling most of the delegates "un-poetic."[124] He also appeared put-off by their strong and often confusing political views, which mostly fit into the communist persuasion. As it turned out, the conference had been sponsored by the country's Communist Party, and it seemed there was as much discussion of political matters as poetic ones. Over the course of his stay in South America, Allen's journals were dominated by political thoughts more than at any other time. His political awareness increased during his stay in Europe, but now he was being challenged even further, and he constantly asked himself what his true views were. The local communists took him to visit a mine, where Allen witnessed the harsh lives of workers who struggled for eleven hours a day for just a dime an hour.

Ginsberg was keen to show off his language skills, and so he delivered speeches in English, French, and Spanish, and also took his chance to spread the gospel of the Beat Generation. Back in America, he had argued vociferously with the media over their conflation of "Beat" and "beatnik," and here at the poetry conference he took his chance to persuade an international audience of his definition of the movement. He delivered a long lecture on the Beats and read his own poetry, along with works by Corso, Philip Lamantia, and John Wieners. "I think it was probably the best of the speeches," he later said, rather immodestly.[125] He seemed to view his efforts as successful, stating, "Beat Generation is considered great new American poetry and all the professors will bring it back to Uruguay and Argentina and perhaps Colombia."[126]

Although the Beats were known around the world by now (Louis Ginsberg had proudly told his son that he'd heard about people in Moscow reading Ginsberg's poetry), this was Allen's chance to bring the Beat Generation to the world on his own terms. He had viewed this trip to South America partly as an escape from his duties as Beat Generation spokesperson and literary agent, but for the first week of his trip at least he was keen to spread his poetic ideals. This in itself is interesting because during all of his previous journeys abroad, he had seemed more interested in finding time or inspiration to write, and seeking out other poets, whereas now he was actively spreading the word of his own poetic peers. He was also busy as always networking with other poets, including fellow City Lights author Nicanor Parra, and believed that he had scored an all-expenses-paid invitation to visit China with Peter, although this fell through and he didn't get to visit China for another few decades.

When the conference finished, Allen took a third-class sleeper train heading south for Chiloé, an island in the south of the country, where he intended to "eat fish and maybe finish Kaddish."[127] He had been trying to make final edits to his latest collection for City Lights, but was having trouble with it. However, in Chile he found a new perspective on his poetry by speaking Spanish constantly, and was able to simplify his language more through thinking in a second language instead of his native English. He stopped off in Temuco, and then in Valdivia. Here, however, he fell sick and had to stay put until he recovered. Whereas most of Chile reminded him of California, Valdivia made him think of New Orleans. A network of rivers joined in the middle of the city, and everywhere you looked there were barges and boats, and you could hardly get anywhere without being ferried across the water.

By 9th February Allen still hadn't gotten to Chiloé,

but he had made it to a small, scenic town called Calbuco that overlooked Chile's southern islands. He stayed with a local poet called Hugo Zambelli, and went out on the fishing boats with the local fisherman. He ate local delicacies that he'd never even imagined before and saw penguins swimming alongside fishing boats. The town was a beautiful little place that reminded him of a Brueghel painting, but best of all, he was now very much free of the Beat Generation. Although he had come to Chile to spread word of his peers' work, he had quickly grown weary of being a world famous poet, and was now enjoying his anonymity.

Instead of continuing south to Chiloé, after two weeks with Zambelli he headed east to the border with Argentina, crossing over and travelling through the Andes as far as San Carlos de Bariloche. This, he thought, must be the most beautiful landscape in the world. For about a week he explored the mountains and lakes before returning to Santiago in early March.

By now he had spent longer than intended in South America and his roundtrip ticket had expired. In order to extend his stay, he gave a lecture at the University of Chile for forty dollars, which left his ticket open for another few months. The lecture gig was set up for him by Nicanor Parra, with whom Allen had been staying. Although Parra was friendly and hospitable, they eventually got on each other's nerves and argued over politics. Parra's left-wing leanings were too much even for Allen Ginsberg. Eisenhower was also in town and Allen managed to see him deliver a speech. He noted that the president "talked weird" and got mixed up in the middle of his sentences.[128] While in Santiago, Allen had the peace and quiet required to work on his *Kaddish* manuscript, and was delighted to meet yet another literary celebrity, the celebrated poet Pablo Neruda.

After two weeks in Santiago, Allen made his way to the next country on his list, Bolivia. After sending Ferlinghetti his amendments to *Kaddish*, he received a cheque that allowed him a bit more freedom to travel. However, the cheque was accompanied by a note warning him away from La Paz, which Ferlinghetti called the "dung hole of humanity."[129] Unfortunately, Allen's ticket was already booked, and La Paz was his next stop on the way to Lima, in Peru.

Although he only intended to stay a day or two, La Paz wasn't as bad as Ferlinghetti had said, and he decided to stay longer. Allen was immediately taken with altitude sickness, which is hardly surprisingly considering that it's the world's highest capital city, and he spent his first day in the city lying in bed with a crippling headache. He stayed in a one dollar room at the Hotel Torino and once he recovered he spent his time exploring the winding streets of the city, buying little trinkets in the market from colourfully-dressed Indian women with babies on their backs. He also purchased some Chinese scrolls and shipped them back to New York, thinking they were a smart investment.*

He had planned to take cocaine but instead settled

---

* He also bought some pottery which he believed would be worth a small fortune back in the U.S. At this point Allen was starting to feel the passing of time and was clearly looking at mining his travels for some sort of investment in his future.

for coca leaves—the raw ingredient used to produce cocaine—which stained his mouth green and made his breath stink. All around him was a staggering poverty that left him feeling very much out of place, but he did his best to fit in and ate at local street stalls. However, his bravery in eating local food backfired on him as he developed what he described as a "rare disease of the ass" which took the form of a tumour.[130] It cost him forty dollars to get it supposedly cured by a doctor, but Bill Morgan, in his biography of Ginsberg, speculates that it was a complication stemming from this illness that killed Allen some forty years later. Certainly, from this point on his travels would be marred by ill health.

As well as seeing most of La Paz, during his weeks in Bolivia Allen also explored Lake Titicaca and a small town at the foot of Mount Illampu, called Sorata. "It is strange how real Bolivia is," he noted in an unpublished poem.[131]

His next destination was Peru and in particular Machu Picchu, so-called "Lost City of the Incas," that had been brought to international attention only fifty years earlier by the American explorer, Hiram Bingham. He sat in the back of a crowded truck full of Indians for twelve hours to Puno, on the Peruvian side of Lake Titicaca, and from there took a train to Cuzco. Machu Picchu reminded him of Palenque in Mexico, and as he had done in Mexico, he again lived with the local caretaker in a shack overlooking the city ruins. He followed the trails around the mountainside for about a week and sat out under the stars at night, exploring the temples and tombs by moonlight.

Then he took off for Lima, Peru's capital city on the Pacific coast. In 1953, Burroughs had written that the area around Lima was "dead and empty as the moon" with vultures "wheeling overhead as if they were waiting for all Lima to die." Yet that was just Burroughsian hyperbole. He also acknowledged that it was a highlight in his own South American itinerary, being comparatively free from Spanish influence: "Lima is pure South America, a city like no other place on earth."[132] He had also reported that it was the best place for sex with young boys since he visited Vienna in the 1930s. Allen stayed at the Hotel Comercio, near the train station, for about three weeks, studying Incan archaeology and sampling the local drugs, including ether. He took a whole bottle of it and wrote a poem, called "Aether." The experience reminded him of laughing gas, which had given him a near religious experience during his last stay in the United States. The laughing gas incident had had such a profound impact upon him, in fact, that over the course of many years he was obsessed with seeking out new substances around the world to give him insight into the world and his own mind, and this was very much a preoccupation of his during the South American trip. But it wasn't just ether that Ginsberg was eager to try.

During his own travels in South America, Burroughs had tried a little-known drug called yagé or ayahuasca—an ancient brew made from the Banisteriopsis caapi vine. "This is the most powerful drug I have ever experienced," he remarked.[133] Although not trained as a botanist in any sense, Burroughs had taken his quest for yagé seriously and embedded himself in a scientific research party, finally acquiring the drug and impressing the scientists with his willingness to consume it so readily. He had written extensive letters home to Allen about his experience, saying that "yage (sic) is space time travel"[134] and writing long passages about its effects as though providing him access to some sort of universal consciousness. Ever since Bill reported on its effects in a series of letters, Allen had been interested in trying it for himself. Even Ferlinghetti had managed to find some during his brief trip to Bolivia. Now, as Allen travelled South America wrestling with his ego in the light of his newfound fame, he was keen to experiment with yagé and see what it could do to him.

Through Peter Matthiessen, a founding editor of *The Paris Review*, Allen was able to procure a half gallon of yagé in Lima, which he then took in his $0.40 hotel room. He noted the results in his journal:

> Slowly drifting away but still thinking in my body, till my body turned to passive wood and soul rocked back and forth, preparing to slide out on eternal journal backwards from my head in the dark.[135]

He knew that this was not the full yagé experience, and that to get the real effect of the drug he would need to go into the jungle and try it in its original preparation with the local *curanderos*, or witch-doctors. So a few days later, he took off by train and bus through

Huánuco—which Burroughs had warned was "an awful dump"—and Tingo María for Pucallpa on the Ucayali River. Parts of the journey were incredibly slow, and he found himself stopped for a few days in small towns, again wandering the markets and eating at cheap Chinese restaurants.* The last leg of his journey was in the back of a truck, lying on top of a mountain of sugar, staring up at the stars through the dense jungle. It was the beginning of June and he had been on the road all alone for more than four months, and as he moved further and further into what seemed like the middle of nowhere, he viewed himself as "a permanent traveler."[136]

In Pucallpa, Ginsberg befriended a *curandero* called Maestro, who gave him his first real taste of yagé. He drank the brew like beer and lay back in anticipation. After forty-five minutes, he felt "the Great Being" approach him "like a big wet vagina."[137] Embracing the experience, he conjured up an image of a black hole and entered through it. For the next two and a half hours, he hallucinated colourful snakes that appeared very real to him. The whole trip was far more powerful than the one he'd had in his hotel room, and when it was over he met with other people who had taken yagé with him that night and felt "a great feeling of communal fraternity and a sharing of a realisation of Infinite Intimacy."[138]

Allen was captivated by his yagé trip and spent the

---

* Everywhere both Burroughs and Ginsberg travelled in South America, they seemed to find Chinese-owned businesses, many of which operated twenty-four hours. Fortunately, both of them loved Chinese food.

next day working on a poem about it—"Magic Psalm." In this poem, which was heavily edited and appeared in *Kaddish and Other Poems*, we can see the poet moving towards a belief in a universal consciousness that had been slowly growing through the marriage of his travels and drug experiences. The poem is also more experimental than any of Ginsberg's previous work, reflecting the incredible effect that yagé had had on his mind. During this month, and at some point after taking more yagé, Ginsberg also wrote "The Reply" and "The End," which both made it into *Kaddish and Other Poems*, and both concern his yagé experiences. In particular, "The Reply" makes references to visions Allen experienced the next day.

The following evening, Allen returned for another dose of yagé with the *curandero*, this time receiving the "full ceremony" that involved smoke being blown on the freshly-brewed drink. Just prior to the effects taking control, Ginsberg looked up and saw a shooting star and the full moon, then lay down in anticipation of a similarly pleasant experience to what he'd encountered the night before. Instead, "the whole fucking Cosmos broke loose" and he was thrust into "the strongest and worst" trip of his life. He later noted that it was far more intense than even LSD. The visions and ideas he had were intense and bizarre: "We are God's vomit, he vomited out consciousness out of himself into our Being in order to be conscious of himself."[139] The colourful snakes he'd seen were now crawling all over him as he vomited uncontrollably and was made aware of his own impending death and the death of everyone he knew. He saw another man in the group, but could see right through to his skeleton, and thought of his own death and the suffering it would leave upon Peter and his father, and thought of his mother's pain prior to her passing.

Although the experience traumatised him, Allen stuck around in Pucallpa to take yet more yagé. It was the only drug that brought him into this dark area of his mind that allowed him to explore death, which terrified him. He felt that it was worth the risk, even though he was told that unlike other drugs, to which one builds a tolerance, every dose of yagé became more powerful than the one before it. And it was not just death that he feared. "I hardly have the nerve to go back," he wrote Burroughs, saying he was "afraid of some real madness, a Change Universe permanently changed."[140] Unfortunately for Allen, Bill was now deep into Dianetics and Cut-ups and his response offered little in the way of practical help or sympathy for Allen's terror.

Ever eager to explore his own inner-self and the wider universe, Allen didn't shy away from going back, in spite of his fear. The effects on him were significant. For one thing, after seemingly speaking to god, he decided he wanted to have children and make love to women again.* For another, he came to an understanding of life that matches well with Buddhism, which he had previously studied a little, but that he

---

* This was not just a sudden onset as a result of the yagé. He had mentioned a yearning for sex with women in his journals throughout the journey.

wouldn't truly understand for another few years. Life is suffering, he realised, and "the purpose of life is death." The combined experiences pushed him towards an understanding of the universe as entirely inter-connected, and he even learned to empathise with the mosquitoes that were biting him: "We are all trapped in the Divine Honey, like flies, struggling in different ways to accommodate ourselves."[141] He wrote his father to say that "the universe did seem like one Being."[142] Although there was much terror, he also learned a great deal from each experience.

In addition to these insights into his own psyche and what he felt was the nature of the world or even god, Ginsberg's inquest into yagé was also scientific, and indeed much more scientific than Burroughs', although it didn't seem that way to either of them. Both men viewed Burroughs as the scientific adventurer and the truly knowledgeable one on the subject of South America and yagé, but Allen did more reading, spoke to more experts, and came away with a better under-standing of how yagé worked. For one thing, Burroughs left with the idea that yagé was a single vine, boiled into a brew. Allen, however, realised that it was the combination of two or more substances that triggered the effects they'd both experienced. Burroughs made more generalisations and relied more on hearsay and intuition, whereas Ginsberg spoke with more people and asked probing questions.

One of the people to whom he spoke was Dr. Binder at a nearby hospital, who directed Allen to a remote village in the jungle, accessible by boat on the Ucyali

River. After ten days in Pucallpa, he hopped a ride on a riverboat for the one-thousand-mile journey to the Amazon River, taking around a week. He slept in his hammock on the deck, watching the jungle pass by. Every twenty or fifty miles they passed a cluster of huts, and every hundred miles a small "frontier town."[143] The trip cost a mere six dollars, and whenever the boat stopped it allowed him the opportunity to get out and explore these odd little settlements in the jungle. Finally, they stopped at a town called Iquitos, where he met a new *curandero* called Julio Maldonado. His experiences here were much the same as in Pucallpa. He took it another four times, making it eight times in total.

Allen had originally planned on a series of boat journeys across more than two thousand miles of South America to the Atlantic Ocean, but by now he was feeling homesick after six months of very solitary travel. He was also lacking the necessary funds (about fifty dollars, at least) to continue on down the Amazon, and so instead of pursuing new adventures, he flew back to Lima on his still-valid plane ticket, gained permission from the authorities to export the yagé samples he'd collected in the jungle, then visited Panama very briefly, where he tried the drug soma, and flew home to New York City. Robert Creeley was in Guatemala and Allen was interested in visiting him, but this wasn't the time for further travel. Six months alone had given him time to think and write, and the yagé had pushed him further into his own head. It was time to get back with the people he knew and loved.

Allen's journey through South America had proven very useful in terms of his development as a writer. In thinking so much in Spanish, he had learned to simplify his poetry somewhat and stop being so wordy. He had also regularly encountered new experiences, and so filled dozens of notebooks with his observations. "Every time I sit down there's a new town to describe in diary," he said to his brother.[144] Normally, during his travels, he wrote many letters to friends and family, but in South America he was working on his poetry, and managed to produce an entire book of poems during his six month trip. The yagé experience had opened his mind and given him insight into the universe, as well as new possibilities in poetry. It had also fuelled his curiosity for trying more drugs.

Perhaps of greatest immediate significance was that he had more or less finished *Kaddish and Other Poems*— which he considered his best work—and even added three new poems to it based upon his drug experiments. Published the following year, 1961, it was a book made almost entirely of poems written while travelling or inspired by his experiences outside America. Most of it was written in Paris, and the final three poems in Peru. The perspectives gained simply could not have been found if he had not travelled so widely and with such openness to experience. Back in America, he had been too distracted by the business of being a poet to actually write much poetry.

In the middle of 1960, Allen returned to America after yet another long voyage. By now he had seen huge chunks of North America and South America, a vast swath of Western Europe, and a little of Africa. Each journey had changed him and prepared him for the next. His trips had shaped his perception of the country to which he kept returning, of the world as a whole, and of himself. By now he was sporting a thick black beard and talking about universal consciousness. He had two hugely important poems under his belt and a wealth of experience with psychedelics. It was the dawn of the sixties, and Allen Ginsberg was about to become one of the decade's most important and recognizable figures. His experiences as a traveller had made him into this countercultural icon, and yet he still had one more major journey to make that would finally mould him into the Allen Ginsberg the whole world would know.

Part Three:
The Change
1960-1963

"India is the greatest nation of earth and wild as it's rumoured, and everyone's turned on to the cosmos."

Back to Europe

When Allen Ginsberg arrived back in America in June, 1960, he was met by a stack of three hundred letters that had piled up in his absence. South America had been a rare break from this sort of correspondence, and he quickly became depressed being back home in the role of Beat Generation spokesperson and all-round literary celebrity. When one of the letters turned out to be from Gregory Corso, who invited him back to Europe, Allen decided that his stay in the U.S. would be short-lived. He had already set his mind on Asia, but now he was planning a longer journey, starting off in Europe and not returning to America for a few years. In Part Two we read about Ginsberg's ability to survive for extended periods abroad, but now he had in mind a journey that would be far longer than any he had yet undertaken. He didn't know where he was going, but he knew he wanted to see India above all else. He felt it was one place he could be anonymous again, as he had been in South America. He also knew that in India he might be able to find a new perspective on the world through a combination of spiritualism and drug-use, as in America, despite a growing interest in psychedelics, the authorities at least were becoming increasingly anti-drug. His yagé visions had given him more questions than answers, and he was keen to get out and explore further.

The U.S. was also distressing him politically. His travels had given him a perspective on American politics that made actually living there quite unpleasant. He felt a profound anger at the U.S. government, which pushed for censorship of poetry, yet interfered in the politics of sovereign nations, sold arms to dictators, and ordered executions in the United States and elsewhere. He wrote a poem called "Subliminal" that angrily compared the crimes of poets to the atrocities and potential atrocities committed by the American government around the world. Politics dominated his poetry, his journals, his dreams, and his letters. He argued with his father and wrote constantly on the evils of the American government and its interference around the globe. In a letter to Corso from September, 1960, he lists twenty-seven grave injustices for which America was responsible, and many of them involved crimes perpetrated on other countries, including places Allen had visited or was interested in visiting:

> 3. Run South American governments for their
> own benefit for 50 years
> [...]
> 8. Stopped democratic govt in Guatemala
> 9. Support Franco in Spain
> [...]
> 11. Started worldwide hysteria against benevolent
> Narcotics
> [...]
> 13. Support Chiang Kai-shek dictatorship in
> Formosa
> [...]
> 17. Prevent free change of travel to China[1]

His political leaning at this point was partly communist, and he had strong sympathies for China, the Soviets, and Cuba, as well as the places he'd visited in South America that had outspoken communist movements. It was clear that he was neither comfortable nor welcome in America. Even his friends and family seemed far removed from his political views. By the time he set out on his next great journey in March, 1961, he had written in his journal:

> But I have tried to speak
> to this unholy nation
> and my spirit weakens &
> sees only its own death . . .[2]

Unsurprisingly, the one big problem he had that stopped him from taking off when he wanted to was a lack of funds. However, Allen always said that money materialised when needed, and in this case it certainly did. The Poets Foundation unexpectedly sent him a cheque for a thousand dollars, and he quickly took off for Europe with Peter.

On 23rd March, 1961, Allen and Peter set off for France on the *S.S. America*. As they knew it would be a few years before they returned, there were many friends and family on the dock to wave them off. Allen felt that it was "like we were going to another planet."[3] It was also snowing, and Allen watched the skyline of New York vanish into the mist and snow as they slunk off into the Atlantic Ocean. Peter quipped, "I hope America will still be there when we get back."[4] It was as though he'd read Allen's mind.

On 1st April, after passing close by the Irish coast, they arrived at Le Havre and took a train to Paris, where they once again checked in at the Beat Hotel. Allen had hoped to rendezvous with Burroughs, but Bill had taken off just before the pair arrived. He had given no explanation for his disappearance, but Brion Gysin, an odd man who held considerable sway over Burroughs during the sixties, explained that it was because Burroughs was keen to avoid Allen and Peter. Like many others, Ginsberg found it difficult to tolerate Gysin, but did so long enough to find out that Burroughs was in Tangier.

After a few weeks in Paris, Allen made his way by train to Cannes for the film festival, where he rubbed shoulders with the stars, took lots of heroin, and spent a few more weeks exploring the area. He had been invited by the director of a movie called *The Connection*, and everyone involved on the project was staying in a large house for the duration of the festival. Ginsberg, Corso, and Orlovsky were given the basement. In May, they went to St. Tropez and spent two weeks with Jacques Stern, again fraternising with "movie stars and spies".5 Despite the exotic location and having everything bankrolled by his rich friend, Allen was once again uncertain about his life:

> a famous personal American in the Port
> of Saint-Tropez among the rich
> eating lobsters & scotch and worried about
> my figure in a cute blue bikini—
> with all my problems solved except

what am I doing here
and what next for kicks on earth
except India and later death[6]

He visited nearby Marseille and Aix-en-Provence, where he saw Montagne Sainte-Victoire, the mountain famously painted by Paul Cézanne in a long series of paintings. He bought a postcard reproduction of one such painting and compared it to the real thing, "measuring each brushstroke to a geological epoch."[7] Then, Allen let Stern pay for his boat trip through the Mediterranean to Tangier on the *S.S. Azemour.* On the boat, he wrote the poem "Sunset S.S. Azemour."

They arrived in Tangier on 1st June, but Corso's passport had expired and so Allen accompanied him to Casablanca for a replacement. They got back to Tangier two days later, intending once again to stay for a long time. As Gysin had suggested in Paris, Burroughs' feelings towards Allen seemingly had turned sour. He had become deeply paranoid, developing a strong dislike for Peter, and was even suspicious of Allen. While Allen had been promoting Burroughs' work and writing the blurb for his latest novel, Burroughs hadn't even bothered to read *Kaddish*. Under Gysin's influence, he was experimenting with an artistic form called "The Cut-ups," and had gone as far as to cut up his own personality and perceptions. The change in Burroughs was deeply traumatic for Ginsberg, who later remarked that "if I don't know Bill then I don't know myself because he was my rock of Tolerance and Friendship and true Art."[8]

Their old residence, the Hotel Muniria, was now too expensive for them, and so Allen, Peter, and Gregory took rooms very near at the Hotel Armor for just twenty dollars per month. Corso's was cheaper but larger, while Allen and Peter had a rooftop overlooking the bay and the "parapets of Spain."⁹ Food was cheap, too. Allen noted that it was cheaper even than Mexico. The atmosphere had improved since the last time as tensions had settled down in the few years since it became part of Morocco, and in their first days there it seems everything was peaceful and tranquil as Allen and Peter enjoyed drinking mint tea under fig trees and looking out over the sea. In Tangier, Allen was able to write a bit, but he was still sometimes overwhelmed by literary business as letters piled up, consuming whole days as he attempted to reply to them all. He complained to his father: "I wonder how I can get out of this Allen Ginsberg trap."¹⁰

The highlight of Ginsberg's stay in Morocco was a trip to Marrakech—"the maddest teahead city I've ever seen"¹¹—where he stayed for several weeks with Paul Bowles. It was a pleasant trip for Allen, who enjoyed the quiet inland life that was more authentically Moroccan than Tangier, and felt at peace lying out on the roof at night under the stars near the Koutoubia Mosque, smoking copious amounts of hashish. Beneath Bowles' balcony lay the town's main marketplace, which inspired Ginsberg's poem, "Djemâa el Fna in Marrakech." He learned some Arabic here and wrote joyous descriptions of life in this beautiful part of the world, before taking a first-class train back to Tangier.

Life in Tangier was not so enjoyable for Orlovsky, who had quickly grown miserable. First he had gotten sick, then he had been mercilessly bullied by Burroughs and Burroughs' friends, and finally he had fallen out with Allen. In July, Orlovsky took off for Greece alone, intending to travel the Middle East by himself. Allen was sad, but felt they would meet up somewhere in a matter of months or years, and that they would be happy once again.

Bill and his young friends were planning a trip to England, and although there was still animosity between them, Allen intended to tag along. However, by August he had changed his mind. Corso took off and Ansen, who had been visiting for the summer, returned to Venice, leaving Allen all alone. He felt rejected by those who loved him and was now also feeling old: "I am 35 and half my life now past, I have no sure road ahead, but many to choose from, and none seem inevitable."[12] After nearly two months of "incomprehensible petty jealousies and horrors," he had had enough of Tangier and decided to catch up with Peter in the Middle East. So, on 24th August, at 2 pm, he sailed out of Tangier on the *S.S. Vulcania*, headed for Athens via Palermo and Naples. From "the gates of Hercules"[13] he intended to visit the Acropolis and the Sphinx before reaching India, by unknown means, in time for Christmas. As he stood on deck, watching Tangier disappear into a "blue mist," he thought himself "alone, solitary, hopeless, tranquil, still with knapsack."[14]

Greece and the Middle East

Allen's trip to Greece was not just in the hope of eventually meeting up with Peter again. The country was the birthplace of democracy, as well as western literature and philosophy. Ginsberg's travels thus far were not just conducted for the pure joy of travel, but to learn from the places he visited, and he was often drawn to places whose ancient cultures contained what he anticipated to be valuable lessons. In Europe he had been in his element among the old buildings and classical works of art. In Latin America he had soaked up Mayan and Incan culture through carved stones. Naturally, Greece drew him towards it with its ancient ruins. Moreover, his friends had visited, and at least some of them pushed Allen to go as well. Burroughs had travelled to Athens to marry a Jewish woman in 1937; Ansen had visited during the fifties and been so impressed that in the sixties he would move there permanently; Corso had fallen in love with the country, writing countless poems about the wonders of classical Greek culture. Even Louis Ginsberg, who had never been there, wrote passionately about how wonderful Greece would be to visit.

Ginsberg arrived in Athens late and spent the night walking around the capital, talking to people he met in cafés. He was immediately taken by the city, and would go on to enjoy his travels around the rest of the country, despite the persistent sadness he felt at what had happened in Tangier. His Greek journey began inauspiciously as he had only three dollars in his pocket that first night. Corso, who had visited Greece some two years earlier, owed him money, so when morning came he went to the American Express office to collect what had supposedly been sent to him. However, the ever-unreliable Corso had not bothered to send anything. He'd been gambling at casinos all around Europe and had lost everything. Allen wrote an angry letter, pointing out that Corso owed him more than $200, and Gregory soon sent what he could afford—just $14. Thankfully, a cheque soon arrived from *Show Business Illustrated* for an article he had written, which was never published. This helped Allen fund a two-month stay in the country, giving him plenty of time to explore.

Starting off in Athens, which Allen wrote was "like a small town and very cute and toylike,"[15] and where he took in all the tourists sites, smoked pot on the Acropolis, and ogled the statues of naked boys, he then travelled with newfound friends to Delphi. The bus ride there was spent incredibly high on pot, staring out the window at "Town roofs stretched from the shore to the wrist of blue water,/ opening bayward with paths of water inland, straits & coves & round small Islands."[16] At Delphi, he spent four days with a local poet called Angelos Sikelianos and climbed Mount Parnassus half-naked, and then took the train to Olympia. The journey to Olympia was "hideous," Allen noted in his journal, as he vomited repeatedly in the train toilet and suffered from a terrible headache.[17] Following his Hachette guidebook to Greece, he explored the famous Temple of Zeus and admired the Hermes of Praxiteles statue, noting various details but focusing mostly on the genitals.

He returned to Athens by ferry to collect his mail, and then took off again for Hydra, Epidaurus, Nafplion, Mycenae, and Argos. In Hydra he ogled a young boy who reminded him of a childhood crush, Paul Roth, and in Epidaurus he climbed the hills and admired the ancient amphitheatre. At Nafplion he "went goo goo eyed with amaze on top castle of the Franko Turkish Venetian castle rampart fort on top of hill" and explored yet more fortresses and ruins at Mycenae and Argos. As he had done elsewhere on his travels, he was not just armed with a guidebook, but also more scholarly texts like *Mycenae: An Archaeological History and Guide*, which helped him to better appreciate the landscape and ruins that he found across Greece. He also put his traveller skills to the test by simply wandering around and sitting with strangers to pick their brains about things to see. As always, he managed to transcend linguistic barriers and connect with people.

By early October, Ginsberg was back in Athens and had a healthy social life with many artistic Greek friends, and was having lots of sex. He was also quite impressed by the modern culture of Athens, as well as having obviously been enamoured by its history. "Greek music and dancing is the loveliest outside of US blues I ever heard," he told Gary Snyder.[18] To Lawrence Ferlinghetti, he wrote that "Greece is really Greece, everybody's sexy and the light's immense."[19] He also loved that the local boys would dance to the music almost as a form of prayer, "unlike [in] hardhearted America."[20] Next, he took off for Phaistos on the island of Crete, where he spent nearly two weeks and read Homer's *The Iliad* and *The Odyssey*. On Crete, he visited Heraklion, Malia, and Aghios Nikolaos. He was impressed by the beautiful landscapes and did much walking and climbing, including a hike to Dikteon Andron, the mythical birthplace of Zeus. In the cave, he stayed until night fell and watched an old Austrian man catch and preserve moths, before descending the hill by flashlight, contemplating death. Despite his adventures and his appreciation for Greece's "idyllic valleys," he was depressed through most of his time there. Back in Athens by mid-October, he was writing poems about loneliness and death again.

> I hear mustaches whistle behind me.
> My dreams whistle at me in bed,
> When I'm dead I hope the bones
> Don't start whistling in the graveyard.[21]

Even his observations of the beautiful places he saw were coloured by death: "The light thru Parthenon columns is a great white-blue solid color—like looking thru eyesockets of a skull."[22]

Throughout his time in Greece, Allen planned his onward travels. He still anticipated being in India, although he now also wanted to include Ceylon (now Sri Lanka) in the itinerary, on the advice of both Paul Bowles and Gary Snyder. He still wanted to see Egypt and other parts of Africa, as well as Syria, Persia (now Iran), and elsewhere in the Middle East. Of course, he was also eager to meet up with Peter, a desire which trumped everything else in the short term, and so on 26th October he set sail for Israel.

Ginsberg anticipated that Orlovsky's mother would send him a V.A. disability cheque to Haifa, and so Allen headed there. He cried as the ship came into port, suffering what he called "old holyland blues."[23] When he couldn't find Peter, Allen spent a somewhat solitary few weeks exploring the region around Haifa, visiting Galilee to see some of the places mentioned in the Bible and meeting up with relatives. He also tried to see the Wailing Wall in Old Jerusalem, but at this point in history it was in Jordan, and Allen was not able to travel there. (It was returned to Israel during the Six-Day War in 1967.) "Israel is an interesting drag," he soon decided.[24] Despite having previously felt connected to the country by his Jewish ancestry, while actually in Israel he was less impressed.

> The main beauty of Israel . . . is that it is a haven for persecuted Jews . . . I don't personally feel much historical connection in my bones after all—I feel it more in the Idea or Ideal than I do in the reality while I'm here . . . as a matter of fact I feel a more pronounced tendency to feel at home among Indians & Arabs in Mexico or Tangier . . .[25]

In his letters and journals, he observed what he considered foolish political and religious differences that caused terrible problems throughout the Middle

East, and which impacted him personally. He wanted to travel to Egypt but couldn't because it was an Arab nation. He wanted to see Iran and Jordan, but couldn't for the same reason. He wasn't even allowed to write a letter to a friend in Morocco because it was yet another Arab country. Allen despaired of the Jewish state, and felt like an outsider:

> Haifa is like a ratty looking Bronx, amazingly full of Jewish people who all think they're Jewish, under a Jewish sky with Jewish streetcars and Jewish airplanes and armies and Jewish speeches and dances and theatres and Jewish newspapers, so after a while I felt like an Arab. Except like being surrounded by millions of relatives from Newark, so I felt lost and lonely.[26]

During his travels in both Greece and Israel, Ginsberg thought a lot about politics and Cold War meddling by both the U.S. and the Soviets. In Greece, the intellectuals told him about the police state and oppression of political dissent, and in Israel they lamented the anti-Arab prejudices. He noted in his journal a woman describing all Arabs as drug addicts, cowards, and possessing an "inferior mentality."[27] The political situation, mixed with his interactions and travels in Israel, inspired some more poetry as Allen filled his journals with vitriolic poems railing against the C.I.A. and F.B.I, capitalism and communism, and asking what exactly constitutes a "just war."[28]

He was alone until mid-November, when he finally met up with Orlovsky in Tel Aviv. During his lonesome travels in Israel, Allen had sent him many letters but gotten no replies. Peter, meanwhile, had travelled through Greece, Turkey, Syria, Lebanon, Jordan, and Egypt before visiting Israel in search of Allen. The time apart had been good for Peter, and he was ready to travel with Allen once again as they set their sights on the long-awaited trip to India.

Although they managed to squeeze in some tourist activities like floating on the Dead Sea, visiting the parts of Jerusalem that were then in Israel, and visiting Sodom and Eilat, they found Israel terribly expensive. When Allen met up with Peter, they had just $300 between them, and in December they were stuck in Acre, awaiting a $500 cheque from *Playboy*. They no longer had the luxury of choosing their next destination based upon their desires, but instead were faced with difficult choices limited by the Jewish state's spats with its neighbours. They could fly out of the country, but how would they afford it? Worse still, India would only give visas to people who could prove they had the funds to support themselves during their stay, as well as a pre-booked ticket out of the country. Things were looking bad, and Allen's goal of being in India or Ceylon by New Year was now more or less impossible.

Back to Africa

After two months, Peter and Allen finally left Israel by ship on 28th December, 1961, and, after a brief stop in Massawa (which was then in Ethiopia, but is now a part of independent Eritrea) arrived in French Somaliland (later known as Djibouti) on 3rd January. When Allen first visited Africa in 1947, he had Rimbaud on his mind, and now he was visiting the Horn of Africa, where Rimbaud had lived and worked prior to his death. Unfortunately, they found that Rimbaud had lived in Tadjoura, which was a little too far for them to visit during their brief stopover. They did, however, visit the capital's main marketplace, which had been called Place Arthur Rimbaud since 1938. Six days later, they arrived in Dar es Salaam, in Tanganyika (which later became known as Tanzania), and spent a few days digging the "independence fever."[29] A month earlier, Tanganyika had secured its independence from Great Britain, but a year-long intermediary period saw the country transition from colonial rule to full independence under the auspices of a governor general. They then sailed north to Mombasa in Kenya (then a British colony, but also on the cusp of independence), where they could apply for their Indian visas. They arrived on 12th January, having been at sea for more than a fortnight, but they were not able to get their Indian visas until February. Despite having intended to be there before Christmas, 1961, the Indian visit was pushed back again and again, and Ceylon was now entirely off the cards.

Still, Peter and Allen were together and Kenya

proved "a very exciting & curious human scene" which they really enjoyed seeing.[30] Mombasa was cheap and pleasant, with marijuana readily available, and they were able to get out and explore the country. They visited Kilimanjaro, stayed a while in Nairobi, and saw Massai warriors. They also crossed back into Tanzania again by bus. From the bus window, as they rolled across the vast country, Allen reported seeing lions, giraffes, zebras, and ostriches. They even saw a vast political rally held by Jomo Kenyatta, the first prime minister and president of Kenya, as the only white people in the audience. It was, he reported, "a weird dreamlike experience."[31] During the rally, Allen had his wallet stolen, but it was all so much fun that he didn't even care too much about the theft. Still, he observed the political situation carefully and decided that while Israel's problems all stemmed from religion, in Kenya it was race that caused tensions between people.

As they waited for their Indian visas, Peter and Allen read books about India and watched Indian movies to prepare. They returned to Mombasa and stayed at the Hydro Hotel, waiting patiently.

India

Ginsberg had been thinking about a trip to India for almost a decade before he set off from Mombasa on the *S.S. Amra* to Bombay (now Mumbai) on 6th February, 1962. He had long admired Whitman's poem, "Passage to India," not just for its anaphora but for its celebration of the spiritual wisdom of the East and "pre-dict[ing] a meeting of Eastern and Western thought in our twentieth century."[32] The prospect of visiting India greatly excited him. He had spoken to people like Paul Bowles, who had visited, and Gary Snyder, who was there, as well as reading countless books to get a feel for the country that he expected to provide him with spiritual nourishment. In Israel, in November, he had even begun dreaming about India, which he started to call the "promised land."[33]

Their boat journey cost fifty dollars and took thirteen days, passing through the Pakistani capital of Karachi and arriving in Bombay on 15th February. It was horribly crowded on board, but Allen and Peter had bunks next to an air hatch and managed to enjoy the trip. Allen passed the time reading Rudyard Kipling's *Kim*, a novel noted for its vivid portrayal of life all across India in the late nineteenth century, and E.M. Forster's *Passage to India*, which explores racial tensions between the Indians and British in the 1920s.

They arrived in Bombay with just one dollar between them, but thankfully Ferlinghetti had sent Allen's most recent royalty cheque, which they exchanged for rupees. With this money, they took a cheap hotel room and waited to hear from Snyder and his wife, Joanne Kyger. For two days, Allen and Peter explored Bombay, taking rides in horse-drawn carriages through the crowded city streets and eating vegetarian meals for just fifteen or twenty cents. After two days, having heard nothing from Snyder, they travelled north by train to Delhi, the capital city. The train journey itself proved pleasant as they reclined on air mattresses, ate delicious food, and watched the exotic landscape pass slowly by. A Jain businessman on the train let them in on an important travel tip that they would make great use of during their time in India—in all the towns and cities throughout India there are large dormitories called dharamshalas that provide free accommodation and sometimes even free food. "I never saw a place more convenient for wandering and traveling," Allen soon reported.[34] Armed with this new knowledge, they checked into a big dharamshala called the Jain Rest House on Lady Hardinge Road, in Delhi's old city, and again waited to hear from Snyder and Kyger.

Unbeknownst to any of them, Gary and Joanne were actually staying just a few blocks away, but it was only on 25th February that they finally met up. Allen and Gary hadn't seen each other in six years, as Snyder had been living in Japan. They spent the next week exploring Delhi's sights, from the Red Fort to the mosques and temples. Allen's love affair with Indian music began in Delhi when he watched the famous tabla player, Chatur Lall, play a concert. In fact, it was during his time in India, and likely beginning with this very concert, that Allen's own musical ambitions began to show.

India was everything Allen hoped it would be and more. Despite his voluminous reading prior to arriving in the country, it was overwhelming to actually be there. He compared it to Mexico and South America in terms of filth, poverty, and overcrowding, but these things weren't off-putting for him. Rather, he found himself absolutely enamoured of it all. There were "billions of people like nowhere I seen," he commented, all stuffed into "crowded streets full of barbers and street shoe repairmen and bicycle rickshaws and Sikhs in turbans and big happy cows everywhere stealing cabbages from pushcarts."[35] Allen had gone to India seeking anonymity and he enjoyed blending into the crowds. Even as a white man he didn't stand out very much with his shoulder-length hair, vegetarian diet, and "Indian Gandhi-style shirt & pants made of handloom cloth." He said, "I look exactly like an Indian native."[36]

Kyger described him (and Peter):

> Allen Ginsberg is running around in an unwashed white Indian (grey) pajama outfit with flapping arms and legs, or else very short shorts from Israel, and a Greek shirt and red nylon socks. He is balding on top, his curling hair down his neck. But if you think his hair is long, you should see Peter Orlovsky whose hair actually falls over his face to his nose in front (but that's all right because he can take drugs behind it easier) and down to his shoulders in back and a tee shirt that doesn't quite cover seven inches of his stomach in front and some tennis shoes full of holes without any shoelaces. The Indians for their own perverse reasons seem to adore him.[37]

Now that they had met up with Gary and Joanne, the four Beat poets headed further north into the foothills

of the Himalayas for two months of spiritual exploration. They first stopped at an ashram, which is a sort
of monastery, near Nanda Devi, India's second highest
mountain. Here, they met Swami Shivananda, whom
Allen described as a "charlatan of mass-production
international nirvana racket—but actually quite a calm
holy old man."[38] Despite feeling that Shivananda was a
fraud, Allen still learned a great deal from the meeting.
As Snyder explained to him, even the fake holy men
have something to teach. It was very much as he had
read in Kipling's *Kim*:

> All India is full of holy men stammering
> gospels in strange tongues; shaken and
> consumed in the fires of their own zeal;
> dreamers, babblers, and visionaries: as
> it has been from the beginning and will
> continue to the end.[39]

The experience at Shivananda's ashram was hugely
important for Allen. The swami gave him a book called
Raja Yoga for Americans, which was Allen's first proper
introduction to yoga—something he would continue to
study throughout his time in India and beyond. Allen
also learned the Hare Krishna mantra and went on to
be one of the first people to popularise it in the West,
chanting it at readings and protests when he returned to
America. Already Ginsberg was learning and changing
just as he had predicted, and having suffered a crushing
depression following his last visit in Tangier, he was
now happy once again. Shivananda may have been full

of bullshit, Allen noted, but he was preferable to "all that Tangier austerity and loveless gurus."[40]

After leaving the ashram, they walked along the Ganges, finding a group of sadhus meditating in perfect stillness. Allen was amazed, but shortly after a boy in orange robes claimed the sadhus were nothing compared to the "real yogis whom you can't see back in the mountains."[41] They saw yet more sadhus at a festival held once every twelve years in Hardwar, which very much impressed Snyder.

They pushed on further to Almora and Dharamsala, from where they hiked way up into the mountains. Along the way, they passed the Dalai Lama's heavi-ly-guarded home. They made an appointment and the next day were allowed into the residence to speak with him for an hour. Snyder, who was well-versed in the religious traditions, greeted the Dalai Lama by pros-trating himself, but the other three used more western style greetings. They asked a great many questions, but Allen managed to annoy Gary by speaking too much about drugs. The Dalai Lama answered Ginsberg by explaining that hallucinations are genuine psychic ex-periences but are not entirely useful because they are achieved too easily. Instead, one should focus on the process of attaining the experience. This was another important discovery for Allen, who had previously been somewhat obsessed with attaining profound psychic experiences and wisdom through drug use. In Israel, he had already begun to feel differently, noting in his journal:

> Thought of getting psychedelic high is a
> disturbance . . . Yet I been talking Tran-
> scendency to everyone from Morocco to
> Palestine. Endless jabber about drugs, like
> the Ancient Mariner with his albatross.[42]

However, here in India he was hearing it from the highest authority. Although he would continue to experiment with drugs in India and occasionally after returning to the U.S., he would no longer rely upon them so heavily, and his personal view of their validity for spiritual purposes would more closely match what he was told by the Dalai Lama. In 1965, he explained that "the Asian experience kind of got me out of the corner I painted myself in with drugs," referring to his obsession with seeking a recreation of his 1948 Blake vision.[43]

Ginsberg's questions to the Dalai Lama irritated both Snyder and Kyger, the latter feeling that Allen's spiritual quest in India was largely fraudulent. She felt Allen wanted to be "instantly enlightened" and that "he actually believes that he knows it all, but just wishes he *felt* better about it."[44] There were small arguments between the group, of course, but the ill-feelings that Kyger had for Ginsberg and Orlovsky ran particularly deep. Kyger felt that Allen mostly ignored her, which is probably true. She is largely absent from his journals and photos, and this is true of many of the women he met on his journeys. If they are not entirely ignored, they are certainly not given as much attention and value as the men he met.

While Kyger assessed Allen as a know-it-all, in fact he was wracked with self-doubt and even self-loathing at times. Wandering around India, he sought lessons everywhere and tried to learn meditation and yoga, but felt he was never going to be any good at these things. He tried learning from experts, but their competence just made him feel worse.

> There's no direction I can willingly go into without strain—nearest being lotus posture & quiet mornings, vegetarian breathing before the dawn, I may never be able to do that with devotion. And if it is a matter of Karma and reincarnation, when will I ever learn? All the saints like Shivananda handing me rupees & books of yoga and I'm no good. My hair getting long, wearing a huge thin silk shirt, useless to perfect my conscience.[45]

Allen had had a crush on Snyder since they first met and, in contrast to his apparent dismissal of Kyger, he heaped praise upon Snyder, whom he viewed as virtually a holy man. Gary was able to teach Allen about the various religions they encountered, instruct him in meditation, help him with yoga, and wherever they went Gary's actions were treated with reverence by Allen in his journals and letters. When they travelled to Faridpur to see the Ajunta caves, Allen was impressed when Gary chanted sutras in Japanese with his "sepulchral voice."[46]

After viewing more caves at Ellora and Aurangabad, where Allen saw carvings that he felt put even Michelangelo to shame, and after exploring the Buddhist, Hindu, and Jain artefacts there, the four weary travellers returned to Bombay in mid-April. There, they stayed with Pupal Jayakar, a woman Allen had known in New York. She had a large, luxurious house on Malabar Hill, where they lived in comparative luxury. After two months' hiking in the mountains, they were served breakfast in bed and could take hot showers. The news from home, though, put an abrupt end to the happiness that had come from their voyage through India. Allen's former girlfriend, the poet Elise Cowen, had killed herself, and Allen felt a degree of responsibility; Jack Kerouac was quickly descending into worse depths of alcoholism; and Peter's brother Lafcadio was doing badly in the mental hospital, with his mother blaming Allen for his violent insanity.

In Bombay, Allen read widely, connected with Indian intellectuals, gave interviews to the media, and even did a few public readings with Peter and Gary. After Gary and Joanne took a boat back to Japan on 21st April, Allen and Peter stayed in the city for another month. Despite the bad news from home, they were relatively happy there. Peter fell in love with Pupal's daughter and also frequented the local prostitutes, whose prices were absurdly low. Morphine could be bought over the counter in any pharmacy, and both men were taken by the opium dens, with Allen writing that "it's a new kick I never experienced and I thank the kindly gods who reserved that charming surprise for my middle age."[47] All around them in Bombay, as well as north in the mountains, it seemed to Allen that weirdness was not only tolerated but celebrated. It was a rare place where someone like Peter was not considered remotely strange. Allen wrote Paul Bowles to observe that "Indians really sophisticated as far as letting everybody be as crazy as they want"[48] and thought that his intellectual friends from around the globe would be happier in such an environment. Despite being considered somewhat normal in India, Peter had to do a test to confirm he was crazy enough to continue receiving disability cheques from the U.S. government. He passed with flying colours.

Summer was approaching and they heard that Bombay would be unbearable in the heat, so they embarked upon a fifty-two hour train ride across the country to Calcutta, and then Allen headed back into the Himalayas alone to explore further. In the far northeast of the country, not far from the border with Nepal, he visited the mountain cities of Darjeeling and Kalimpong. Here he experienced some success in meditation, tried to learn tantra, and then met with a Tibetan lama called Dudjom Rinpoche, who gave Allen some of the most important advice he ever received. In response to Allen telling him about his fear of hallucinations whilst on drugs, Dudjom simply explained: "If you see anything horrible, don't cling to it. If you see anything beautiful, don't cling to it."[49] The message was not immediately clear, but he later realised how much he had been clinging to the Blake vision. Building upon his meeting with the Dalai Lama, Ginsberg was finally moving away from the influence of that pivotal moment in his life. Later that summer he would finally realise how much effort he had put into chasing the Blake vision through drug use, and how pointless it had become:

> . . . I realized how much of my life I'd put into this sort of exploration of mind thru drugs, & how sad & futile I felt now that I had gotten to point with hallucinogens where I no longer liked what I felt & was too disturbed and frightened to continue.[50]

Allen briefly left India to visit the country of Sikkim, which later became an Indian state. He "saw all sorts of Holy Lamas and heard about how monstrous the Chinese were in Tibet."[51] The Tibetans there, he decided, were "the most interesting people on the face of the earth."[52] He met with yet another Tibetan lama, Gyalwa Karmapa, who promised that in a week of teaching he could show Allen some really important things. However, after losing his papers and being unable to acquire a full tourist visa, Ginsberg only had a three-day pass to visit Sikkim. He wanted to return in autumn with a bag of psychedelics but never did, and deeply regretted missing out on whatever Karmapa would have taught him. He left the country deeply annoyed, heading back to Calcutta for the Durga Puja holidays in mid-October. Although in India Allen had broken his obsession with using drugs as an easy gateway to enlightenment, he still very much enjoyed using marijuana, and partook during the Hindu festival.

He also smoked pot when he visited the burning ghats, which are where bodies are burned beside the river. Yet another of the major transformations to beset Allen during this trip was the experience of witnessing these bodies being burned and the ashes turned into the river. Following on from the lesson not to "cling" to good or bad visions, he was learning not to cling to himself or his body. He watched all kinds of people being set alight and saw their flesh and bones in the flames, and he realised that they were already gone. "Amazing how after a few visits one realizes nothing is happening except a lot of old sofas and pillows of meat are being disposed of," he explained to his father.[53] Elsewhere, he called them "meat dolls" and noted that the bodies were essentially "empty" now that life had left them.[54] In India, death seemed to be everywhere that Allen looked, and not just as a philosophical concept; rather, people often just lay dead in the streets. For six months he spent time at the ghats, smoking weed, talking with sadhus, and watching corpses burn as his fear of death was carried away in the smoke that drifted up into the sky. He took photos of severed arms and legs and sent them to Gary Snyder. He even spent whole nights watching and learning how the Indians dealt with something that he had feared his whole life. They were not sad at the supposed loss of a loved one, but instead they were joyful at this new transition. The effect on Allen's worldview was monumental.

As Allen grew more accepting of death, he wrote his first will—a paragraph in his journal bequeathing his literary estate to Peter. During the unrelenting summer heat, in their filthy hotel room, Allen was beset by a range of health problems. Now in middle age, he was not just coming to understand death but actually contemplating his own mortality as his body seemingly began to fall apart. He caught the flu, got kidney stones, worms, heat fatigue, dysentery, and bronchitis. He also had allergic reactions to some of the medicines given to him as a cure for his illnesses. During his travels he was often sick, probably due to the rough nature of his trips and the cheap food he ate. In India, he even drank unfiltered water, which people told him "was instant death."[55]

As with most of the places he travelled, India was having an effect on Allen's political outlook. He told Kerouac, "I think wandering around outside U.S. does enlarge perspective."[56] Through Europe and South America he had been developing his ideas on global politics, coming closer and closer to being the peace-loving hippie idol of the sixties, but it was in India that this transformation finally came about. All his ideas about the evils of the U.S. government and the Cold War were being processed in the context of the spiritual revelations that came with his various experiences throughout India. For weeks, he became obsessed with nuclear war, and corresponded with Bertrand Russell, who told Allen that nuclear annihilation was inevitable. Their correspondence unfolded while the Cuban Missile Crisis played out, with Allen developing some of the ideas for which he would later be widely known. Although he expressed confusion and uncertainty in his letters, he also suggested utilisation of mass media for raising public awareness to influence governments against moving the world closer to destruction. Over this period he grappled with the question of whether to sit back and watch the situation unfold by itself, hoping for the best, or to attempt an intervention by means of protest, or to challenge what he perceived as war-mongering propaganda in the press. We can see during his time in India his position shifting from an aggressive stance against the U.S. government and others to a more peace-loving outlook, as he wrote Kerouac that he hoped everyone—even war-mongering politicians—ended up in heaven together.

His ideas on poetry, too, were undergoing a process of change. Near Darjeeling, a female lama told Allen that his visions and hallucinations were "all illusion."[57] Although he was not one to take advice from women very seriously, this seemed to confirm what other wise people had told him, and he took it to heart. On Peter's birthday, back in Calcutta, Ginsberg wrote a long descriptive sketch of a trip to a Chinese opium den and then rewrote it as a very short poem, boiled down to its essence. Both pieces of writing are the clearest and most interesting of his journal entries in India, and seem to harken back to lessons from Kerouac in the forties. Yet in a short explanatory note after these journal entries, he explained his newfound beliefs and how they guided him to this style of writing. He first explained the development of science, painting, and music in the twentieth century, before getting to poetry:

Now poetry instead of relying for effect on dreaminess of image or sharpness of visual phanopoeia—instead of conjuring a vision or telling a truth, stops. Because all visions & all truths are no longer considerable as objective & eternal facts, but as plastic projections of the maker & his language. So nobody can seriously go on passionately concerned with *effects* however seemingly real they be, when he knows inside all his visions & truths are empty, finally. So the next step is examination of the cause of these effects, the vehicle of the visions, the conceiver of the truth, which is: words. Language, the prime material itself.[58]

He describes his new style as influenced by Kerouac's poetry, as well as Burroughs' "random jux-taposition" or cut-up method, which had previously depressed Ginsberg, as it appeared to mark the death of poetry. Now Allen is more interested in "imagistic photo descriptions," although he acknowledges in the next sentence, "I really don't know what I'm doing now."[59] He goes on to question the rigid structures by which poets are constrained, referring not just to line length but whether or not it is reasonable to have lines run from left to right on the page. "We think in blocks of sensation & images," he notes, suggesting that poetry could better reflect the "shape" of the mind of the poet.[60] In a letter to his publisher, Lawrence Fer-linghetti, he said that he wanted to find a "change in composition as violent as cut-ups" but that he hadn't yet figured out exactly what he wanted to do.[61] Although he continued writing left to right and started usually at the margin, many of the poems in his *Indian Journals*, published in 1970, were very experimental and pushed him in a new poetic (and political) direction.

In Calcutta, Ginsberg was busy working on the proofs for his next book, *Reality Sandwiches*. This was a collection of poems from the period 1953-1960, excluding those already used in *Howl* or *Kaddish*. Ginsberg called it his book of "writings from Mexico & So America & travels."[62] Indeed, the book can be viewed as an insight into the evolution of Allen's poetic methods as influenced by his major travels in the 1950s. Even the publicity text places strong emphasis on it having been written in far-flung locations, and in Allen's biography (both of these he wrote himself for City Lights, his publisher), he lists his various travels:

High school in Paterson till 17, Columbia College, merchant marine, Texas and Denver copyboy, Times Square, amigos in jail, dishwashing, book reviews, Mexico City, market research, Satori in Harlem, Yucatan and Chiapas 1954, West Coast 3 years. Later Arctic Sea trip, Tangier, Venice, Amsterdam, Paris, read at Oxford Harvard Columbia Chicago, quit, wrote "Kaddish" 1959, made tape to leave behind & fade in Orient awhile.

The very first poem is called "My Alba," and begins: "Now that I've wasted/ five years in Manhattan". It is followed by a poem about a painting that was very influential on him, "Sakyamuni Coming Out from the Mountain." The painting was something he found in 1953, when his obsession with Asia really began. Next are poems about travelling America ("Green Automobile"), Cuba ("Havana 1953"), Mexico ("Siesta in Xbalba and Return to the States"), Peru ("To an Old Poet in Peru" and "Aether"), and even a poem about air travel ("Over Kansas"). Others are written at sea ("Tears") or allude to dreams or plans about travelling ("Ready to Roll"). When Ginsberg is writing back in the U.S., he is looking out at the world, referencing places he has been or wants to go. Through the book, a playfulness with form develops until, in the final poem, all conventions are very much shattered as he writes from a Lima hotel room, spreading words all over the page in differing sizes and making odd shapes with the text. It seems likely these poems were composed from journal entries while Allen was going through his latest poetic phase in India.

By September, 1962, Ginsberg had been in India for seven months and was low on funds, looking for a way to stretch out his travels. Allen always claimed that, when travelling, money would materialise when he most needed it, and once again that happened as Robert Creeley offered him an open-ended round-the-world plane ticket in exchange for reading at a poetry conference in Vancouver. This meant that he could afford to stay in India much longer, and even continue his travels onwards into other countries. At the time, he was planning to see Snyder in Japan, to visit Russia, see Australia, and get back to his family in New York and friends in San Francisco. He also expressed an interest in visiting Tashkent, in Uzbekistan, which was then a part of the U.S.S.R. He initially viewed his return to the U.S. as a very short stop to visit his father before returning to Asia, possibly "for a year in Japan."[63]

Although it may seem that Ginsberg was disgusted with life in the U.S. because of his increasingly hostile views towards its government and his determination to spend as much time abroad as possible, in reality he was just enjoying his exploration of the world, which he considered a vital part of his "education." He wrote to Ferlinghetti to explain:

> I'll be here for a year more, traveling—and then a year in Japan—and then back to the states for a year—and then (finally) I wonder if I'll go to Russia and China. The Red countries is the one place I've really missed—part of a twentieth century education I'm lacking.
> [...]
> Well, as I say I will come back to the U.S. as soon as finish my postgraduate course in the world scene—I'm just traveling to improve my education not to escape U.S.A. life which I enjoy, I'm not an expatriate.[64]

They stayed in Calcutta about five months, becoming familiar with the city and integrating with the local intellectuals, before taking off for Benares (which is now known as Varanasi) on 8th December. Benares is considered the holiest city by Hindus and Jains, and is where Buddhism began after the Buddha's first lecture was given nearby. According to Allen, it was untouched by western civilisation, although he was clearly exaggerating as it had by then more than a century of at least minimal contact with western cultures. He also believed it to be the oldest continuously inhabited city in the world, but there are cities more than a thousand years older that have been continuously inhabited.

They rented a hotel room near the Dasaswamedh Ghat for $9 per month, in which chicken wire covered the windows to keep out the mischievous monkeys that lived nearby. They were just a few metres from the Ganges, and Allen, who enjoyed blending with the locals, would squat on the steps to wash his clothes in the river. This proximity to the water reminded him of Venice. He continued visiting the ghats, making extremely vivid notes in his journals and letters about the burning bodies. Here, rather than the local intellectual set, Allen and Peter befriended the beggars and naked sadhus that inhabited Benares' streets. They even went to great lengths to save one poor man who had been mutilated and was on the cusp of starvation. They managed to rescue him, admit him to a hospital, and get in touch with his family. Allen attempted to set up a system for rescuing other people who found themselves homeless and dying on the streets of Benares.

At Christmas time, they took a trip to Agra and its famous Taj Mahal, where, in those simpler days, he was allowed to sleep inside the building for two nights. Allen thought the Taj Mahal was humanity's greatest creation—a "Glorious white dome, hanging in the sky."[65] He smoked a large amount of ganja—as he did in most places he visited in India—and it helped him better appreciate the "infinite sensation" of being in such a majestic place. It was, he said, "the most stupendous motel in the Universe," and he wrote a beautifully descriptive eponymous poem detailing the intricacies of the architecture.[66] He said it had a greater impact on him than the Acropolis "or anything in Rome," while Peter compared it to the pyramids.[67] They then spent time in Brindiban, birthplace of Krishna, where Allen tried to study bhakti yoga. There, he was told that he should look to William Blake as his guru and stop his quest for a living one.

Back in Benares in the first week of January, 1963, Allen gave a free poetry reading at Benares Hindu University. Afterwards, an uptight professor approached him and attacked Allen for using vulgar language. Ginsberg protested, saying that attacking his poetry was the only vulgar thing, and this incensed the professor, who called upon his friends and colleagues. They sent a copy of *Howl* to the Criminal Investigation Department with all the obscenities underlined, hoping that Ginsberg would be punished. The C.I.D., as it turned out, were already investigating Ginsberg and Orlovsky. They were suspicious as to why these Americans were living like poor Indians.

Allen and Peter were thereafter the victims of an odd and cruel campaign of harassment, wherein people from the C.I.D. came to their apartment unannounced to poke around, spied through their windows in the middle of the night, and spent days spreading vile rumours about them to their neighbours. This went on and on until eventually their visa renewals were refused and they were told to leave the country immediately or face a prison sentence. Eventually, a trip to Delhi resulted in the situation being resolved. The two men had their visas extended for six months and apologies were made to Allen and Peter for the harassment. The local Communist Party had been the ones who issued complaints and set in motion the whole affair. Allen, who had learned so much in India, once again took a valuable lesson from this otherwise unpleasant experience. Referring to the professor who had initially accosted him, he said, "I really should treat people gentler and not insult and drive them into a corner so they claw out in self defence."[68] Through this lesson, coupled with his yoga training, Allen was able to move on with his life with much greater self-control and increased patience for others. He related this lesson to the hostility between India and China and the peace marches that were turning violent. He wanted everyone to share his lesson and be able to hold their tempers in check.

Allen continued to make trips from Benares to other parts of India, including Buddhist sites at Bodh

Gaya, Rajgir, Nalanda, Rajagriha, and Patna, where he stayed with the poet, Malay Roychoudhary. At Bodh Gaya, he found an interesting carving of a three-headed fish that thereafter he would use as his personal logo. However, he was spending less and less time with Peter. They had different circles of friends now, as well as different interests. Allen was looking forward to moving on from India to see other places with his plane ticket from Creeley, but Peter wasn't happy with the plan. He called Allen a washed-up sell-out and moved out of their shared room. On 20th May, Allen set off on a train journey to Calcutta alone. He waited a few days before taking a flight out of the country. "No escape but thru Bangkok & New York to Death," he wrote on his last night in India.[69]

Ginsberg had spent fifteen months in India, the "greatest, weirdest nation of history," and arguably they were the most important months of his life.[70] Bill Morgan explained, "Ginsberg initially went to India out of mere curiosity, in search of some peace and quiet, but it turned out that the experience completely altered his life and work."[71] Indeed, he had learned more and changed more than he had in any period prior to this. Yet all the lessons he had learned and all the changes he had undergone were still new and confusing, and his journey was not yet complete. He wasn't about to fly home just yet, and in the last stages of his journey he would have time to fully process the Indian experience.

Catalysing the Change

On 26th May, Ginsberg flew from Calcutta to Bangkok, intending to see a bit of Southeast Asia. His ticket let him stop off almost anywhere in that part of the world for free, and he hoped to see a few different countries, including Burma, Cambodia, and Vietnam. "I'd like to see the war there," he explained.[72] But his first port of call was Thailand.

Although Bangkok is now the most visited city on earth, back in 1963 neither Thailand nor its capital were familiar names in the West. The U.S. had military bases there, and G.I.s were allowed to take leave in Bangkok, but for regular tourists it was not yet the go-to destination it became just a few decades later.

As he did almost everywhere he went, Allen subsisted on Chinese food and wandered around with his guidebook in hand, taking in the museums and statues. In Lumphini Park, he sat under a statue of King Rama VI while the local youths hung out listening to rock music. Two of these boys provided Allen with sex, but he remarked to Orlovsky in a letter: "they stick to me like adhesive tape afterwards."[73] In visiting the Chinese restaurants he had broken months of vegetarianism and in having sex the boys he broke almost two years of celibacy. One of the boys he met also provided him with a supply of morphine.

Next, he flew to Saigon (which was later renamed Ho Chi Minh City) on 31st May. The puppet government, which was propped up by the U.S., was being protested in the streets at this point, and a few months later the unpopular President Ngô Đình Diệm would be overthrown and assassinated. President John F. Kennedy (who would also be assassinated later that year) had been escalating the U.S. involvement in Vietnam, and in mid-1963 Allen found himself in the middle of it all. He spent his four "horrendous days"[74] in Saigon mingling with American reporters, from whom he "got the whole story of Vietnam war gossip" and said "it's like walking around in a mescaline nightmare."[75] He said he was offered the opportunity to go see actual battles in the middle of the country, but he was too afraid. "The war is a fabulous anxiety bringdown. It's *awful*."[76] The reporters, for their part, were bored waiting for a bigger story than the gradual escalation of U.S. involvement and fabricated a story about Allen that ran in the 6th June issue of the *New York Times*: "Buddhists Find a Beatnik Spy."[77]

Although his anti-war views were not fully formed until he returned to the U.S., Allen's politicisation had been on-going throughout his travels, and visits to peace marches in India as well as seeing the build-up of the Vietnam War in Saigon contributed to his views. Almost a decade later, in the early seventies, his anti-war poetry made references to his brief experiences in Saigon and Bangkok. In several poems he referenced the C.I.A. dealing "dope" in Bangkok to fund their participation in the war. In his 1971 poem, "September on Jessore Road," he accuses the C.I.A. of "Smuggling dope in Bangkok's green shade." Ginsberg had spent time in the greenery of Bangkok parks while using morphine.

After the chaos of Saigon, Allen flew to Angkor War, in Cambodia:

> Traveling by jetplane kind of a gas, you do get in and out of centuries from airport hangars & glassy modern downtowns to jungle floating markets & 900 year old stone cities in a matter of minutes & hours instead of weeks & months. Like space cut-ups or collages, one minute paranoiac spyridden Vietnam streets, the same afternoon quiet Cambodian riversides.[78]

Angkor Wat, constructed more than eight hundred years ago, is the world's largest religious monument and has been used as both a Hindu and Buddhist site of worship. It was the capital of the Khmer Empire and although, as some claim, it was never truly abandoned, it did fall into disrepair and was largely consumed by the surrounding jungle until large restoration works in the twentieth century. This must have reminded Ginsberg of his time at Uxmal, in Mexico. Allen spent a week exploring the ruins of this ancient city and was so impressed that on his final day there he wrote a book-length poem about the visit, titled "Angkor Wat." It was later published in 1966.

Although not one of Allen's best known poems, Bill Morgan said that "Angkor Wat" "sounded the beginning of a new fertile period of poetry for him,"[79] while Tony Trigilio compares it in terms of importance to Allen's poetics as "Howl" or "Kaddish,"[80] citing it as a milestone wherein Ginsberg begins fusing Williams' poetics and Buddhist vipassana poetics. "Angkor Wat" is perhaps Allen's first Buddhist poem, yet in it he appears to conflate Buddhism and Hinduism, perhaps as a result of his confusing year and a half travelling India. Some critics have noted this as proof of Allen's lazy approach to eastern spiritualism; however, it is more likely that he was charting his personal development while making reference to the mixed Hindu-Buddhist lineage of the Angkor Wat temples. The poem poses Ginsberg as on a pilgrimage in search of sacred language, which is in a sense what his entire 1961-63 journey was all about. Back in Europe, his father had written him to say, "Soak up impressions like sponge so that you can, undoubtedly, squeeze them out later for new poems."[81] It was somewhat unnecessary advice, as this is something Allen had always done. The trip through Europe, Africa, the Middle East, and Asia had served up not just experiences, but lessons that would shape Allen's personality, politics, and poetics.

While discussing the importance of "Angkor Wat," Trigilio links it to another long poem Ginsberg wrote a month later, tellingly titled "The Change," and written at the very end of Allen's long journey around the world. The day after writing "Angkor Wat," Allen flew to Japan, stopping again briefly in Saigon, and also in Hong Kong. He arrived in Tokyo on 11th June and, as most travellers still feel in the twenty-first century, he was overwhelmed by its modernity. Its cleanliness and development came with a price, though, and Allen couldn't afford to stay at a hotel. Instead, he slept on cardboard outside the train station before catching a morning train to Kyoto. Mount Fuji was obscured by clouds as the train passed by, but Allen had spent so much time examining Japanese paintings that he was nonetheless familiar with it and he cried at its beauty. Though modern Tokyo appeared like a city from the distant future, Mount Fuji was reassuringly ancient.

After a seven-hour ride he met Gary and Joanne and spent twenty hours sleeping at their quaint little home on the edge of the city, recuperating from his travels. Japan was in many ways the polar opposite of India. It was clean and orderly, young couples could walk hand-in-hand, and the crushing spectre of poverty was nowhere to be seen. There were no dead people or beggars on the street, and even the cats and dogs were healthy and well-fed. Soon Allen was immersed in Japanese culture, which proved profoundly different from that in India or Southeast Asia. Thanks to Gary's language skills and guidance, Allen could join Zen meditation lessons, which he found easier and more comfortable than the Hindu style he had tried in India. He learned more in a few days of studying breathing techniques in Japan than he had in a year and a half of wandering through India, hoping to pick it up by proximity to a variety of teachers. In India the religious ceremonies were noisy and colourful, but here in Japan they were almost entirely silent and the monks dressed in black. Gary and Joanne showed him around, introducing him to different Japanese foods, going to teahouses, seeing rice paddies, and even swimming in the Sea of Japan.

Allen's journeys in India had been of unparalleled importance to him and for the most part he had been happy there. Yet in Japan he began to realise that he had also been somewhat depressed. Although the constant presence of death in the streets had helped him get past his own fears, it had also made him constantly think about death, which was not particularly helpful either. The poverty had brought out his charitable side and helped him get in touch with humanity, but it had made him incredibly sad. The filth and noise had made him more tolerant and opened his eyes to the world, but now he was in Japan he appreciated the stark difference. As Allen explored the gay bars of Kyoto and watched the attractive young men and women going about their lives thinking of love and fashion, he didn't forget or regret his Indian experiences, but rather they all began to sink in and he gained a greater perspective. "The depressed humanity brings down the atmosphere, it's real, but it's the Indian universe," he wrote Peter. "Japanese universe much *funnier* and more cheerful."[82] When on his final night in Kyoto Allen ended up in bed with Gary and Joanne, and realised he wanted to have a wife now, it became clear that something inside him had changed monumentally.

The next day, 17th July, on the train back to Tokyo, Allen cried. He always wrote good poetry when he cried, and the result this time was one of his greatest works: "The Change." Throughout his travels he had sought out holy men and gurus and they had all taught him something different, but now Allen could see the messages starting to come together. He felt he had wasted much of his life trying to answer unimportant questions and trying to achieve unimportant goals. He had gotten hung up on visions, the continuation of a pursuit that had begun in 1948 with his Blake vision. Now he realised that what was important was to love himself and others in their present human form, to be open and accepting of everything as it is. On his long voyage he had gone in search of higher conscious-ness, but what he found in the end was that he could be at home in his own body. In 1945, he had confided in Kerouac that "I do not wish to escape to myself, I wish to escape from myself."[83] It was a statement that in many ways remained true throughout his life until the end of this trip as he searched for something outside of his own existence. But in 1963 he realised: "I seem finally to have returned back into my body after many years absence—I think the Indian Gurus did it."[84] The poem that began, "In my train seat I renounce/ my power, so that I do/ live I will die" marked the dividing point in his life. Everything that had come before was a journey of exploration leading to this simple revelation, discovered on the Kyoto-Tokyo Express; thereafter, everything would be entirely different. Allen had been a student of the world, a seeker making his way through more than thirty countries in search of answers and, importantly, in search of himself. Now he had found what he had been looking for.

"The Change" not only reflected the actual change within Allen, which he said "catalysed and precipi-tated" everything he learned on his travels, but also marked a new period in his poetry. Either forgetting or ignoring the eponymous poem written at Angkor Wat (not to mention those that filled his journals from India), he told Snyder that "The Change" was the first poem he'd written "in years." "Thank god I did write one great poem all that time away," he said in a letter from America many months later. He explained to Snyder that the poem "follows mantric-*pranayam-ic*-belly-breathing" which would help readers get into their own bodies as Allen had done. [85] By reading the poem aloud, one would essentially be guided through a meditation. Thereafter, many of Ginsberg's poems and readings would be intended to help his readers and listeners achieve this aim, and he would utilise chants including "OM" and the Hare Krishna mantra at poetry readings for the same purpose.

After his life-changing train ride, Allen spent a few days in Tokyo as he continued to process the lessons he'd learned. He got a handjob from a girl in a bathhouse and realised a secret yearning for women, as well as perhaps a desire to procreate. Beyond just sex, he realised how much he had excluded women from his life. Then, in late July, after more than two years away, he flew back to North America. He had left from the East Coast, travelled through Europe, down to Africa, across Asia, and arrived back on the West Coast. By the time he got back to New York he had fully circumnavigated the global for the first time—a monumental journey that had changed him forever.

Part Four:
World Citizen
1963-1997

"Thru unlimited energy until the age of 38, I had traversed the earth once, and crisscrossed many countries..."

Behind the Iron Curtain

When Allen got back to Canada and then the U.S. he walked around crying. Even when he was teaching in Vancouver, he would start crying. He was not sad, though; these were tears of joy. Back in San Francisco he went "around asking everybody if I can kiss them."[1] He told Gary Snyder that he was in a sort of "happy rapture" and going through a state of "softness" that "lasted for several months."[2] Although he viewed his time in Japan and Southeast Asia as a period of catalysing the changes brought on from India, in reality this extended well into his time back in North America. The "stay in Asia did me a lot of good . . . but effects didn't really take place till I left Japan," he explained.[3]

Originally, Ginsberg had intended on a quick return to Asia, but soon he realised he had gotten everything he needed from his time in India—"namely my own face." Instead, after briefly moving around the U.S., he returned to New York and settled back into the business of being a literary celebrity. He decorated his house with Indian scrolls and other artefacts he'd brought home from his travels and reunited with Peter, who got back from Europe around the same time Allen appeared on the East Coast. They installed a telephone at their house—a first for Allen, and something that became his link to the wider world now that he was settling down for the time being.

The Allen Ginsberg that people saw when he returned was the Allen Ginsberg the public would come to identify with the hippie movement of the 1960s.

He had long hair and a long beard, dressed in Indian clothes, and chanted Hindu mantras wherever he went. He preached peace and love and generally embodied the hippie ethic. "I take no drugs no more nothing but belly flowers," he wrote Kerouac in a long letter that explained his acceptance of himself and everything else in the universe.[4] He became active in literary and political circles, and the Vietnam War increasingly stole his attention as he became one of the faces of the anti-war movement. In Benares, he had attended his first ever peace rally, and he was keen to continue doing so in the U.S., bringing with him his Indian chants to ensure the rallies stayed as peaceful as possible.

Over the next year, Ginsberg stayed put except for small journeys to do literary readings or anti-war protests around the U.S. As always, he was completely broke, but he still had his eyes set on another journey. The Soviet Union was the place he most wanted to go, having planned to visit since his mother's death. Even when he had no money, he was busy planning out a passage to Eastern Europe and beyond. He wrote to Lionel Trilling in 1964 that he had "not been in Eastern Europe before & been everywhere else so it's about time. Might even do east-west relations some good."[5] Still, he had no idea how he'd raise the funds to get there.

Soon after, another communist nation presented an opportunity—Cuba. Since Allen's last visit, much had changed. The Castros had been in prison in 1953 but in 1965 they were running the country, and Cuba was now very much an enemy of the United States. That was all fine with Allen, who jumped at the chance to peek behind enemy lines. He had been spreading his message of peace and love around America and now saw an opportunity to heal the bad blood between the American and Cuban governments, telling Snyder that he was "expecting to make it a pacifist anarchist kindly good neighbor policy scene and not angry Marxist."[6] On 7th January, 1965, after some wrangling with the State Department, his visa was approved for a one month visit. First, though, Allen had to make a brief trip back to Mexico City, as direct travel between the U.S. and Cuba was forbidden.

On 15th January, Allen bid farewell to his brother Eugene at J.F.K. airport and flew back to one of the most significant locations in his life. Although he was sick with grippe, he spent several days trying to relive old experiences. He took in the sights and smells that were so familiar still, and then visited the Chapultepec Park Museum. As with everywhere he travelled, he sought out famous works of art, and here he enjoyed seeing the paintings of Frida Kahlo. Despite feeling tired and sick, he very much enjoyed his brief return and wrote in his journal: "Life is too short—I want to go back to Mexico and live in Oaxaca like a peaceful bearded sage and eat tortillas for a year."[7]

On 18th January, Allen flew to Havana, and the flight reminded him of seeing Cuba from his ship to Africa back in 1947. Upon arrival, he spent his first night hanging out with some young Beat-type kids on the streets, drinking rum and talking until the wee hours. The following day, he went looking for the places he'd visited on his first journey to Cuba in 1953, even though back then he'd considered it a "horrid" city. In particular, he wanted to find the location where he'd sat and written "Havana 1953," suggesting its importance in his poetic development.

Ginsberg had been invited to Cuba by the Casa de las Américas, an organization founded shortly after the revolution in 1959 to promote relations between Cuba and other nations, to judge a literary competition. A rather left-leaning group, they had invited Allen seemingly in order to show him how well things were going in their country, hoping that he would spread the word back to the youth of America. Indeed, Allen was quite impressed upon arrival, but noted that things in Cuba were "both good and bad." He went on to say, "I was here in '53 and the country is much better off" but acknowledged that it was "a quasi police state with no constitutional protection" where certain groups of people (including homosexuals and artists) were suffering greatly.[8] He wandered around a lot late at night and met with hip young poets, but was still rather disappointed by how tame and repressive the country was. He lamented being unable to find a "big mad cheap poetic café" or indeed any place where people could speak and act freely.[9]

Still, Allen tried to stay positive. He viewed himself as a cultural ambassador and, with other channels between the U.S. and Cuba cut off, he brought Bob Dylan and Ray Charles records as gifts for the country's cultural leaders. Staying at the Hotel Havana Riviera, he spent much of his time doing what he loved—playing the role of tourist.* The Casa de las Américas organized various excursions throughout the country, which Allen mostly enjoyed. Nicanor Parra, with whom he'd stayed in Chile, was also a judge, and together they visited various forts and museums, as well as Ernest Hemingway's home and an alligator farm.

Despite his good intentions, it didn't take long for Ginsberg to get himself in trouble. He often spoke out on the controversial subjects of homosexuality and drug use, suggesting that both were in need of legalisation, and then complained about the unlawful arrest of some young artists he'd met. "I was obviously an embarrassment to my hosts," he wrote his father.[10] He told a friend that "I can't keep my mouth shut . . . I'm too hysterical to be quiet more than a week."[11] He frequently complained about not being allowed visitors in his hotel room, and continued speaking out about uncomfortable issues, even asking if Raul Castro was homosexual at one point.

In his journals, Ginsberg began by writing freely, noting down his erotic fantasies about Fidel Castro and Che Guevara, but soon he was mired in paranoia as it became clear that he was being carefully monitored, and the people around him were in danger of punishment for his behaviour. He felt censored, and even began to censor himself, which he hated. His lectures were cancelled, and gossip seemed to swirl around him as people were talking about outrageous things he had never done. Yet on the radio, the news reported only

* Allen had only heard Dylan for the first time upon his return from India in 1963. The song was "Masters of War" and it brought him to tears.

how impressed the famous American poet was with Cuba's progress. He quickly became fed up with the "insanity of this society",[12] where "the papers don't report anything serious [so] all discussion is done by gossip privately which creates chaos."[13]

After taking some antibiotics, Allen had quickly recovered from the grippe he had when arriving in Cuba, but later got a bad case of dysentery. He was also suffering from anxiety due to the stress of being under such constant scrutiny. Nonetheless, he persevered with his duties as a judge, participated in some cultural activities, and quietly continued to lobby for better treatment of homosexuals. He was interested in spreading Burroughs' cut-up technique to Cuba, demonstrating it to many people he met, and talking about it during lectures he gave to groups of writers. On 10th February he flew to the south-eastern end of the island, where he spent several days. He admired the mountainous terrain, which reminded him of the Andes and Himalayas. His descriptions of the landscape are beautiful, but he was more preoccupied with U.S. bombing in North Vietnam, and how the Cuban version of events would invariably differ from what the U.S. media would present. Up in the hills he visited a school where he learned about how the youth were given Marxist indoctrination to turn them into patriots. The sight and sound of hundreds of young girls singing in "insect unity" about fighting for their country was "the wildest thing I saw in Cuba."[14]

On 16th February, he had sex with a man called Manuel Ballagas. Manuel was one of Allen's young writer friends, and they had been getting closer during Allen's time in the country. The two men retired to a friend's house because Allen was often denied visitors at his hotel, and some of his young poet friends had already been arrested for seeing him there. Ginsberg helped Manuel edit down a long "beatnik style" poem to just "essential 5 lines."[15] They then had sex, and upon leaving the apartment were pleased to find no police waiting for them outside.

Two days later, at 8:25 am, a hungover Allen was awoken by a knock on his hotel room door. He had only gone to bed a few hours earlier, and staggered to answer the door dressed in his Indian pyjamas. Three soldiers entered and told him to pack his bags. They wouldn't let him contact the other poets he knew, or the Casa de las Américas, who had invited him. He was taken to an office in Old Havana, where he met with the head of immigration, Mr. Varona.

Allen's account of what happened that morning differs a little from text to text, but in any case he and Mr. Varona quickly got into a car and made for the airport. En route, Allen tried to establish why he was being deported, but the answers were vague. When Ginsberg asked for exact details, Mr. Varona just said: "We called for you last night but you weren't in." When he pressed further, asking which specific laws he had broken, Mr. Varona told him: "Cuban laws . . . Oh just basic immigration policy . . . also a question of your private life . . . your personal attitudes." He then said, "Too much public life."

He wasn't sure what he had done, but he told his

father that it was "probably for talking too much about marijuana & sex & capital punishment."[16] It is very likely they knew about his relationship with Manuel, and that they had also grown tired of Allen constantly speaking out about controversial issues. Ginsberg felt bad for not having kept his mouth shut because he had not only gotten himself deported and failed to sooth the Cold War tensions, but had most likely caused problems for his friends and sponsors back in Cuba. Punishments for people there would be much harsher than for an international visitor. Manuel Ballagas, for instance, was thrown immediately in jail, although he was soon released.*

In a last-ditch attempt to resolve things, Ginsberg explained that he was in favour of the revolution, but it gained him no sympathy. He suggested that perhaps they'd consider letting him stay another few days as he was already scheduled to leave with the other poet delegates, but Mr. Varona told him, "We have to do things fast in a revolution."[17]

He was put on an airplane headed for Czechoslovakia. On board, the socialist newspaper proclaimed, "In Cuba there is true liberty and revolution." Allen was disgusted. He now thought of both capitalists and communists as a "mountain of dogs."[18]

---

* Manuel told Allen that he'd been deported for talking about marijuana and others suggested it was a political move aimed to hurt the Casa de las Américas, but in later years Allen told the story differently, stating that the actual offense had been protesting the wrongful incarceration of homosexuals. The Cuban press reported that Allen had smuggled marijuana into the country in order to corrupt the youth.

After stopping for fuel in Gander, Canada, Allen's plane carried him to Prague, where he arrived on 20th February. Prague had been brutally oppressed by the Nazis and then the Communists, and its people and buildings were all showing signs of suffering, but Allen was in love with the city. "Prague is absolutely beautiful," he wrote, saying also that it was far more "relaxed" than Cuba.[19] Allen seemed very enthusiastic about life in Prague, and it appears the bad impressions he'd got of communism in Cuba were fading fast. He found that his views were tolerated, all consensual sex between adults was legal, and there was a reasonable level of free speech. He was allowed to give a reading for five hundred students at Charles University, where he freely answered questions about drugs. Fortunately for Allen, he was visiting during a rare period of liberalisation that led up to the Prague Spring of 1968, and he decided that communism couldn't be all that bad. It didn't hurt, of course, that he'd learned his lesson about speaking out too openly in Cuba, and for the duration of his stay he "conducted [him]self discreetly" and made sure to avoid any overtly political statements.[20] He didn't embarrass his hosts and he was able to enjoy a relaxing and stimulating month in another beautiful European city.

In addition to spreading the Beat gospel beyond the Iron Curtain, there was time for Allen to revel in some tourist activities. During his visit, he stayed at the luxurious Ambassador Hotel, for which the government paid, and by day he toured the castles, squares, cathedrals, bridges, and museums with his guidebook in hand. Naturally, he "follow[ed] tracks of Kafka" around the city, visiting his apartment and grave.[21] He also mingled with the Jewish community, attending services at Europe's oldest synagogue. He even found time to visit Karlovy Vary and Bratislava (later the capital of an independent Slovakia) to meet local writers.

In addition to the Czech government paying his way, Allen was also paid for performances of his work over several years at the Viola Café, given a grant by the Writers' Union, and paid for royalties his books had earned there. With all that money, he set his eyes on the most important destination post-India: Russia. It wasn't going to be cheap getting there, as he had to pay for everything in advance of his trip, which cost $17 per day in addition to train fare. He could only afford to pay for four days, but thought the Russians might invite him to stay longer at their own expense, as had happened in Prague, and so he hoped to stay much longer. On 18th March, he began a 48-hour, 1,200-mile train ride "through the snows of Russia" from Prague to Moscow.[22] His journals are filled with beautiful notes inspired by his observations of the changing, wintery landscape. On the train, a man who had visited North Korea and China asked Ginsberg if he was "sympathetic to the people's government" and Allen replied: "I hate all government."[23]

As with Prague, Allen immediately fell in love with Moscow. He explored the city, particularly enjoying Red Square, which he explored on his first afternoon in Russia. He wrote:

Red Square, you powerful,
>   you robot time machine
Standing still at the gate
        of Asia, Doorway into
              Siberia

His father and brother had managed to track down an old family relative called Joe Levy, and they met up and shared "tearful stories."[24] For the first time, Allen got to hear the full story of his mother's family and their escape from Russia to the U.S. He went to the ballet, the circus, the theatre, some symphonies, and explored all the museums and art galleries he could find, including the Pushkin Museum, home to some stunning paintings by Gaugin and Cézanne. As he had predicted, he was soon a guest of the state and bumped up to a nicer hotel room for which the government paid. This time it overlooked the Kremlin and Saint Basil's Cathedral, which Allen thought was almost as incredible as the Taj Mahal. On 23rd March, Ginsberg was in Red Square again to see the Russian cosmonauts who had recently returned from space, and saw the General Secretary of the Soviet Union, Leonid Brezhnev, speaking to the excited crowd.

While drunk, Ginsberg met the poet Yevgeny Yevtushenko, perhaps the most famous poet in Russia at that time. Allen immediately tried to touch the handsome blond poet, and told him, "I love you."[25] Whenever they spoke, they did so in Spanish, as it was the only language the two poets had in common. Yevtushenko told Allen that he had heard many "bad things" about the American poet—namely, his interest in drugs and the fact that he was a homosexual. Allen tried to plead his case, but the Russian explained that narcotics and homosexuality were "juvenile pre-occupations [which] have no importance here in Russia."[26] He said he viewed Allen as a great man, but talking about these issues made him think less of his American counterpart. When the conversation turned to politics, Yevtushenko talked a little more, and admitted to having "unpublishable" poems, but was still somewhat hesitant to speak.[27] Later, after meeting and drinking together several times, they became close friends and could communicate more freely. In addition to Yevtushenko, Ginsberg met with Andrei Voznesensky, who spoke English, and poet-mathematician, Alexander Esenin-Volpin, with whom Allen communicated in French.

In Moscow, Allen was aware that the government was far more totalitarian than in Prague and he was carefully guided in his behaviour so as not to cause any trouble. People from the Writer's Union constantly reminded him to keep quiet on contentious issues. In Prague, he had been able to talk freely about sex and drugs (and had even enjoyed several orgies) but in Moscow he was warned not to say anything controversial, and those with whom he tried to broach the subject resisted. As in Cuba, there was a lot of talk about "good" and "bad" in terms of "the people." Allen quipped: "They see me as a foreigner."[28] To him, such divisions were just absurd. For a while, he felt depressed by the differences and lack of real communication, but then he had an epiphany: "I'd forgot to see everyone around as God, and was seeing them as I thought they insisted, as Soviets."[29] He soon felt happier again.

Allen wanted to see all of Russia, but it wasn't possible to see such a vast place in such a short time, so he settled for a few days in Leningrad (now known as Saint Petersburg), the old capital of imperial Russia. Here he saw yet more Rembrandts at the Hermitage Museum and a road called Nevsky Prospect, which Allen had read about in Nikolai Gogol's story of the same name.

Ginsberg mostly enjoyed his time in Russia, but it was eye-opening and at times a little depressing. As in Cuba, there was little freedom to speak, and so communication between people could be limited even when they spoke the same language. Allen was beginning to realise that communism was as bad as, if not worse than, the system of government he so freely criticised back in the West. Years earlier, he had written "Death to Van Gogh's Ear" as a vicious put-down of the American government, but now he felt it was "cheap" and when reading it for a Russian audience he modified it to include the communists as also culpable in bringing the world to the brink.[30] Elsewhere in his journals, he wrote a short poem called "The Red Universe":

> The Communist Part like a giant snake eating
> its own tail
> its teeth are microphones, loudspeaker eyes
> television scales[31]

On the occasions when he could speak somewhat freely with Russian friends, he noted vast differences between the cultures and laws. When he explained to one poet the obscenity trial for *Howl*, the poet replied, "You live in paradise."[32] In all his global travels, Allen had come to think of the U.S. rather negatively, and yet now he realised how lucky he was to have come from a country where he was free to speak out, with only limited consequences. In Russia, writing a poem that criticised the state could be a fatal mistake.

Staying on in Russia was expensive and complicated, and so on 7th April he headed back to the train station, and bid farewell to his poet friends. Rather than return directly to Czechoslovakia, he decided to visit Poland, another country behind the Iron Curtain.

For the first week of his stay in Poland, Ginsberg was a guest of the Ministry of Culture, and after that he paid with royalties from the Polish translations of his books, as well as some money he received from the government. "Never had excess cash like this before," he wrote in his journal.[33] Unlike in the previous few countries, he was not escorted around and closely monitored in Poland. Staying at the Hotel Europe in Warsaw, he spent around a month mostly alone, wandering the streets, unable to speak the language, but smiling at random people. He did manage to meet up with a few friends he'd made in Paris and Saigon, as well as Voznesensky, who was visiting for a week, and occasionally conversed with strangers in French. Allen made a "rimbaud-ish" poet friend with whom he sometimes drank.[34] His friend had escaped the Warsaw

Ghetto and worked as a journalist in the Red Army, where he stood outside the city and watched the Nazis wipe out his people.

Allen had connected with his Jewish roots in Prague and Moscow, and continued to do so in Poland, where he saw ghettos that had been decimated during the war, and visited Auschwitz. He was also moved by a service at a big Russian Orthodox church, where he saw Jesus Christ in a new light: "Christ seemed acceptable, I don't know why he ever seemed alien, except his monopoly— but no less beautiful than Buddha Vishnu".[35]

Wherever he went he was inspired to write poems based upon his experiences and observations, filling an entire journal with his writings. No longer shuttled around by escorts and shackled by judging duties, he was free to write, and his notebooks are full of dense, beautiful descriptions of his surroundings and the people he saw on the street. He worked on his poetry, writing a first draft of "The Moment Returns."

One night, while drunk at the bar of the Hotel Bristol, he wrote a short history of his travel experiences, starting with his first journey to Mexico (he had missed out the Dakar trip, but came back to it later) and leading up to Poland. It begins: "Thru unlimited energy until the age of 38, I had traversed the earth once, and crisscrossed many countries . . ."[36] He summarizes his experiences and names most of the places he had visited in a quick, stream-of-consciousness passage. The next day, he headed to the U.S. Embassy and renewed his passport, asking for a lot of extra pages to be stapled in. He was in full travel mode now, with his eyes set on further locations behind the Iron Curtain. A few people he'd talked to had also convinced him that he should visit Mongolia, China, Taiwan, and Indonesia.

Although Ginsberg enjoyed Warsaw, a temporary trip to Krakow turned into a lazy last few days in the country. He had planned on returning to the capital, but instead spent most of his remaining time lazing about in the cafés and walking the old streets. He even found a gay journalist to sleep with, and visited one of the few known Rembrandt oil landscapes. After a visit to Auschwitz, perhaps the most famous of the Nazi concentration camps, he moved on to Wroclaw, where he ended his tour of Poland.

On 30ᵗʰ April, Allen arrived back in Prague by train. He met up with friends he'd made earlier and the next day celebrated Majales—the student May Day festival that had been banned for twenty years. Due to the liberalisation of Czech politics, the celebration had been reinstated. By surprise, the Polytechnic School selected Allen as their candidate for May King. At first, Allen was nervous, but his friends reassured him that it was not a controversial choice and that there would be no problems. The festival got into full swing and much wine was drunk. Allen was paraded through the streets and gave a speech in which he said, "I want to be the first naked King."[37] In a giant procession, he was led through the streets accompanied by jazz as he chanted Hindu-Buddhist mantras. He gave a speech to a crowd of 15,000 people and dedicated his title to Franz Kafka. Finally, they reached a park where 100,000 people had gathered to formally elect Ginsberg their King of May.

When it came time to elect the Queen of May, the police showed up and deposed Allen, putting a random Czech student in his place. Allen noted that most of the crowd was too drunk to comprehend, and that those who saw mostly assumed it was a student prank.

Deciding that it might be best if he left the country, Allen asked the Writers' Union to look into whether or not he had any sort of funds available in Hungary. While he waited for an answer, he continued to enjoy himself around Prague, including a few "secret nighttime orgies."[38]

It seemed to Allen as though he was being followed and this feeling grew after his notebook (containing much sensitive information) disappeared. One night soon after, he was attacked in an apparent homophobic assault, but the assailant told the police Allen had exposed himself and then attacked him. It was only when Allen demanded to speak with the U.S. consulate that the police let him go and dropped the matter. The next day, however, he was confronted by the police again. The plainclothes officer told him: "We've found your notebook, if you'll come to lost and found with us and identify it we'll return it to you and you'll be back here in half an hour."[39] At the station, he was told the notebook contained illegal material, and the next day he was in more trouble after the police had sifted through his writings. He had actually been careful in what he wrote, fearful that the police might try something like this. However, there were still many references to sex and masturbation that Allen didn't consider obscene, but the police did. He was threatened with deportation from another communist country, but this time his pleas to go of his own free will were granted. He had wanted to see Hungary, but instead thought it better to leave the next day for London. The police made thin-ly-veiled threats aimed at his friends in Prague, and he left worried once again that he had caused suffering for others as he had done in Cuba.

On 7th May, Ginsberg sat on a plane from Prague to London and for the entirety of the journey he scribbled away in his journal. The result was "Kraj Majales," another major poem. In "Kral Majales," Ginsberg denounces both capitalism and communism, while explaining how he—the King of May—was deposed and deported from his own kingdom. It entirely sums up his position as of mid-1965: a more mature poet with a more developed, nuanced worldview, and a far more experienced traveller. His time in the socialist and communist nations of the world had taught him that his previous worldview – of America as the global villain—was naïve. Now he knew capitalists and communists were as bad as each other:

> and the Communists create heavy industry but
> the heart is also heavy
> [...]
>   and the Capitalists drink gin and whiskey
> on airplanes but let Indian brown
>   millions starve
> and when Communist and Capitalist assholes
> tangle the Just man is arrested or robbed or had
>   his head cut off[40]

Although the police promised to mail him his notebook, they never did. Allen appealed to different U.S. embassies with no success. A great deal of poetry was lost, and therefore this poem marks the only remaining work from this leg of his travels.

After arriving in London, Allen looked up Barry Miles at Better Books. The shop had a relationship with City Lights in San Francisco, which involved sending books from local authors to each other to sell to new audiences. Soon Allen was living with Miles and "made Better Books his unofficial headquarters for appointments and interviews."[41] Miles immediately asked Allen to give a reading at the store, which he did. Although not advertised, it attracted a full-house, including Andy Warhol and Donovan. Ginsberg also sought out Bob Dylan, who was in London at the time, and through Dylan he met the Beatles. When he turned thirty-nine on 3rd June, 1965, Allen asked Miles to invite the Beatles to his "surprise" party. John Lennon, who was a fan of Allen's poetry, and George Harrison both turned up, but quickly left after Allen's naked, drunken antics irritated them.

Ginsberg's reading at Better Books was incredibly popular, and when he realised Lawrence Ferlinghetti was coming to town he decided that it was time for Europe to have its first major Beat Generation literary event. Gregory Corso was just over the Channel in Paris, and Allen's new friend, the Russian poet, Voznesensky, was due in England for a short visit. Better Books had only held about fifty people, but the Albert Hall could hold some eight thousand, and so that was selected as the venue. On 11th June, Ginsberg and friends gave an historic poetry reading to a venue packed full of "hairy youths."[42] It was the middle of the Swinging Sixties, and England was going Beat crazy. The Albert Hall reading would in fact go down in history as an important moment for the British counterculture. Allen, however, felt that the reading was a huge failure, and he even managed to fall out with several of the friends and poets he invited, including Corso and Voznesensky.

Allen was delighted to be back in England again, and in addition to his poetic efforts, he of course played the role of tourist. In London, he enjoyed viewing the paintings on display at the National Gallery, and elsewhere he travelled through Worcester, Liverpool, and Brighton, enjoying the local beer, music, and heroin, and scribbling poems into his notebooks wherever he went. It was in England where Allen wrote the first lines to another of his major poems, "Who Be Kind To." The poem is in a sense the culmination of all Ginsberg's travels up until this point—a life comprised of lessons learned on the road. It comes down to a simple message, one that he had more or less stumbled upon a few years earlier, on the way back from India, and written down in "The Change." It was being kind to yourself and accepting yourself; however, in this case it was expanded out to include everyone in the world. This includes politicians, the people around you on a bus, citizens of cities and countries across the globe, and even "murderers in Mekong/ & Congo." The poem refers directly to more than a dozen different countries and includes the line "let's all make love in London".

Clearly his travels in the Soviet nations hadn't dulled his enthusiasm for free love.

On 22nd June, Ginsberg returned to Paris with Ferlinghetti and Corso. However, he hadn't taken any money for any of the readings he'd done in England and so he was too broke even for the cheapest hotels. The first night they spent just walking around the city, and after that Allen was able to sleep at the Mistral Bookstore, as he had done on his first visit in 1957. He stayed there for a week before flying back to the U.S on 29th June.

Upon his return, he was vigorously searched at the airport on suspicion of being a drug smuggler. He was terrified as the police examined his pocket lint because he'd been given the clothes by a friend in London and had absolutely no idea what they would find. Thankfully, there was nothing incriminating there. When the agents left the room, however, Allen saw papers that listed him as a smuggler of narcotics. Indeed, perhaps unsurprisingly, the F.B.I. *did* have a file on Ginsberg and had been tracking his movements since he applied for permission to visit Cuba in January. Their investigation turned up a somewhat incomplete map of Allen's travels around the globe prior to 1965 (beginning after he applied for his first passport in 1957) and notes that he was known to be "sympathetic" to Castro's government and should therefore be considered "circumspect."43

Ginsberg claimed in an interview with Conan O'Brien that, "I found later, I was put on the 'Dangerous to Security' list by the old queen, J. Edgar

Hoover!"[44] However, while the F.B.I. most certainly was tracking his activities (and even shared their information with the Secret Service) during his time in communist countries, they did not believe he was a danger to anyone. Their files, now available thanks to the Freedom of Information Act, make that very clear:

> The dissemination [of information to various government agencies] is also believed warranted in view of his own professed antipathy toward the Federal Government and its representatives and his self-described background as a left-wing, Russian. As noted in the report, GINSBERG has frequently demonstrated publicly for various causes and is a self-admitted user of narcotics and a former psychiatric patient.
>
> A review of GINSBERG's activities, however, reflects no basis either from a membership or activity standpoint for his inclusion on the Security Index. His activities, while bizarre, have not indicated any direction or being inimical to the interests of the US.
>
> No interview of GINSBERG is recommended at any time in view of his narcotic and sexual proclivities, his psychiatric history and his connections with mass media. It is felt that any interview with him would be unproductive and in all probability could

result in embarrassment to the Bureau through his use of connections in the mass media field to publicize such an interview.

The report notes that Allen had been of interest to the various agencies and even at one point considered watching for the sake of the safety of the president due to his weirdness. However, after being deported from Cuba it appears the Bureau lost interest and closed their investigation. The above conclusions show that they had determined Allen was no threat to national security or the president's life. A few years later, further review of Allen's activities (including much anti-war protesting and pro-marijuana campaigning) led to the conclusion that: "His activities, while extremely eccentric, apparently lack any specific direction."

Yet around the time Allen returned to the United States, information was received by the Foreign Broadcast Information Service in Vienna that listed Ginsberg as a narcotics user. This was forwarded to various agencies, and accounts for why he was stopped and searched on his return to the U.S. It is unclear from where this information came; however, it was probably related to several hysterical articles that appeared in Czech newspapers shortly after he left Prague.

Ginsberg's travels in the socialist world had been in-formative. Not long after he returned, he was asked by Thomas Clark whether his travels had helped to "clarify" his view of the world. Naturally, they had. While Allen had utterly failed to heal Cold War tensions or find any real constructive answers to the problems he had previously perceived, he had certainly built upon lessons from previous journeys. He had developed a more nuanced view of the world, and come to view America in a more objective light:

> I no longer feel—I didn't ever feel that there was any answer in dogmatic Lenin-ism-Marxism—but I feel very definitely now that there's no answer to my desires there. Nor do most of the people in those countries—in Russia or Poland or Cuba—really feel that either. . . The general idea of revolution against American idiocy is good, it's still sympathetic, and I guess it's a good thing like in Cuba, and obviously Viet Nam. But what's gonna follow—the dogmatism that follows is a big drag. . .
> But there's one thing I feel certain of, and that's that there's no human answer in communism or capitalism as it's practiced outside of the U. S. in any case. In other words, by hindsight, the interior of America is not bad, at least for me, though it might be bad for a spade, but not too bad, creepy, but it's not impossible. But traveling in countries like Cuba and Viet Nam I realize that the people that get the real evil side effects of America are there— in other words, it really is like imperialism, in that sense. People in the United States

all got money, they got cars, and everybody
else starves on account of American foreign
policy.[45]

It seems that his time behind the Iron Curtain had
dispelled any notion that socialism posed a solution
to the world's problems, while allowing him to see
that the American system was just as awful. It may
have worked well for some people back in the U.S.,
but it was causing untold suffering across the globe.
Ginsberg's travels had taken him now to dozens of
countries, and it seems that everywhere he went he
was recording his experiences and developing a more
informed, mature world-view that was indeed, as Clark
suggested, "clarified" by travelling through a number
of communist countries.

On the Road in the Late Sixties

Ginsberg returned home to find his apartment
robbed—Peter's Indian harmonium and Allen's type-
writers had been stolen by junkies. He stuck around
for only a week before heading out to California to
buy a VW bus. It was the height of the hippie era and
Allen had been their archetype for some time. Now he
was going to join a generation by living on the road. He
stuck a mattress and an ice box in his van and travelled
America and Canada between 1965 and '67. At times it
felt like he was travelling in a spaceship, but often he
was brought down to reality by flashing blue and red

lights. Just as in Cuba and Czechoslovakia, the police operated an oppressive system designed to intimidate and inconvenience people like Allen. He was constantly stopped and searched for narcotics, but fortunately he kept clean during these long trips.

With $600 he'd been given by Bob Dylan, Allen purchased a tape recorder and on a long journey eastward from California he "wrote" his next big poem, "Wichita Vortex Sutra." He sat in the back of the bus, speaking to himself and recording anything he said that he felt was worthwhile. The result was an important anti-war poem in which Ginsberg continues the inner struggle he felt since he spoke with Bertrand Russell from India, wondering what—if anything—could or should be done to bring an end to war. The poem is infused with Buddhist and Hindu ideas as Ginsberg searches for a language appropriate to spread his pacifist messages:

> I search for the language
> 　　　that is also yours—
> 　　almost all our language has been taxed by
> war.[46]

In juxtaposing fragments of news about the on-going war with his thoughts on language and ob-servations on the road, as well as glimpses of America's conservative heartland, he draws attention to the meaninglessness of words in their present context. As a poet, he is appalled, yet it is his job to reclaim them. The words that have been spoken by media outlets and politicians have created war, yet it is all an illusion, and the right words can make it all go away. What he is searching for through this stream-of-consciousness poem is a mantra that would solve all these problems. He comes to this very conclusion, reclaiming the power of language for the forces of good:

> I lift my voice aloud,
>> make Mantra of American language now,
>> I here declare the end of the War!47

As with most of his post-India poems, breath here is of great importance because it affects actual change. Just as Allen chanted "Om" to calm angry crowds, this poem was intended to calm an angry nation.

In its nearly spontaneous composition, "Wichita Vortex Sutra" harkens back to lessons Allen received from Jack Kerouac, yet it also draws upon Whitman and Blake. In this sense, although it is a new method of poetic composition, it is also a poem that uses older influences. It is therefore important as a work that captures an unusually wide range of Allen's poetic techniques and themes. Another poem begun on the road, it also takes great influence from his travels and reaffirms his citizenship, not of the United States but of the World. As the poem opens, it appears to be a story about the American road, yet it becomes increasingly global as it takes in all humanity, draws upon Allen's discoveries in India, and addresses the war in Vietnam.

Father and Son Visit Europe

The road trip that gave birth to "Wichita Vortex Sutra" took place in February, 1966. For nearly that entire year, and much of the next, Allen travelled constantly around the U.S. to give poetry readings. He travelled and read so much that, according to Bob Rosenthal, he read "Howl" at least once in all fifty states. The travel began to take a toll on him and he sought a break from it. What he wanted was to travel, but to do so on his own terms and in a faraway land where he was seeing new places and having totally new experiences. Even though he now thought of himself as "an old man," he maintained his child-like curiosity for the wider world. He was keen to get back to Asia and see more of India and Japan with Gary Snyder, and also to return to Europe for another, more in-depth trip, but he was too busy. He was still eager to see China, which had eluded him for decades, but this was particularly unlikely as the Cultural Revolution had just begun.

In 1967, Allen cancelled all his readings for the autumn, hired a secretary to take over some of his work, and returned to Europe. This time, however, he wanted to take his father with him. Louis Ginsberg was in some regards a worldly man—he was extremely intelligent and familiar with all the great poets of Europe—however, in his seventy years on earth, he had never actually left the United States. Allen was delighted to take his father to Europe and show him around. In recent years, the father-son relationship had somewhat turned around as Louis began taking advice from Allen on his poetry after Allen's fame had far eclipsed his own.

On 4th July, Allen flew to Italy alone, with his father scheduled to come out after a few weeks and meet him in London. A few days later, Allen attended the opera in Spoleto and was shocked to bump into Ezra Pound, whom he had arranged to meet at some point during his trip. It was just a very brief encounter, and Pound remained completely silent, but Allen was delighted nonetheless. On 9th July, Ginsberg read with Corso at the Festival of Two Worlds in Spoleto. The reading went well, but shortly after, as he waited for a drink in a bar, Allen was arrested and interrogated by undercover police. He was released, but the lawsuit, which was over obscenities in an Italian translation of his work, went on for another five years in his absence.

Next, Allen flew to England to await his father's arrival and also to participate in a poetry conference. Although the trip to Europe was an escape from his hectic reading schedule in the U.S., it wasn't without its work pressures. Still, he enjoyed meeting the other poets and had a great time in London. The highlight of his trip, however, and indeed a highlight of his whole life, was hanging out with Paul McCartney, John Lennon, and Mick Jagger. Allen was invited to watch them record "Dandelion." Of course, the singers all knew of Ginsberg's work and admired him, but around certain celebrities Allen seemed almost like a teenage fan.

From England, Ginsberg travelled to Wales and visited Tintern Abbey, where William Wordsworth had written "Lines Composed a Few Miles above Tintern Abbey, on Revisiting the Banks of the Wye during a Tour. July 13, 1798." Allen dropped some acid and wrote his own version in which he intended to "bring back a poem [from the resulting visions], maybe a poem about God or something".[48] Instead of attempting to describe the state of his mind or trace his thoughts, he simply wrote his observations of the physical world. The result was "Wales Visitation," which he considered one of his finest works. He even read it to William F. Buckley on "Firing Line" the following year. Allen had claimed to have given up drugs like L.S.D. after returning from India but he was open to some further experimentation. It is interesting to note, though, that the trip in Wales resulted in an overwhelmingly pleasant experience. Indeed, he meditated to control his mind, "So my mind became somewhat immoveable and no longer prey to fantasy."[49] Long gone are the terrible visions that plagued his mind when doing hallucinogens prior to his Indian travels. They are also noticeably absent from his poetry. In addition, the Welsh drug trip and resulting poem pushed Allen into a new area of interest: ecology. This would be a major preoccupation of his, as both activist and poet.

When Louis and his wife Edith arrived in London on 16th August, Allen played the role of tour guide and took them around all the famous locations, including the Tower of London and the British Museum. Then they took off for Paris, where they sat on the Pont des Arts, saw Napoleon's tomb, and revelled in the café culture Allen so loved. Next they saw Rome, which was what

Louis most wanted to see. One night, Allen snuck out to meet young men and was picked up by the police. His father had to come and bail him out, which thankfully Louis found very funny. They then saw the Vatican and Venice before Louis and Edith returned to the U.S. The bond between father and son had been strengthened significantly. Allen later wrote of a great sense of pride in being able to show his father "how much I knew of the outer world".[50]

Alone again, Allen continued to tour Italy. This time, he saw Milan, Pisa, Siena, Florence, Naples, and Turin. As always, he took in as many art galleries as he could find, admiring some works by Raphael and Caravaggio. On 23rd September, he managed to finally get his meeting with Pound. As in their brief encounter at the opera, Pound stayed completely silent. Allen was not put off, and waited around for another month until he could see the aged poet once more. On 22nd October, Allen met Pound again. This time he smoked pot, brought records to play, and was more persistent in getting a reply. Pound gave Ginsberg a few short replies, smiling as he listened to Dylan and the Beatles, and Allen stuck around for several weeks, trying further. In the end, he did get Pound to speak. He spoke of his regrets, describing his work as "Stupidity and ignorance," and said "my worst mistake was the stupid suburban prejudice of anti-Semitism"[51]. From his journal, it's clear that Allen's time in Italy was one of his most productive, and it seems the little fragments of speech he got from Pound, and even just being in the older poet's presence, was inspirational for him. It was just another example of how Allen travelled to meet people he admired, and seemed to gain something important just from his proximity to them. Even in his forties, as one of the most famous poets in the world, he still had the same attitude that he held in his youth.

Sporadic Travels

When Allen returned to the United States after more than four months in Europe, he launched back into the exhausting life he'd left behind—anti-war protests and reading tours. In early 1968, he visited thirty colleges in forty days. He began to think about retiring from reading, and in addition to the property he now owned at Cherry Valley, in upstate New York, he also purchased land in the Sierras with Gary Snyder, where he hoped to one day retire in peace. Although he had no intention of ceasing his personal travels, Allen yearned to be free from obligations, and looked to a quiet retirement in the mountains where he could meditate. His East Hill Farm at Cherry Valley had been an attempt to provide a positive environment for his drug-addicted friends, but for Allen it had not really provided much solace. Much of the money he earned giving readings went into paying farm bills. It even became a source of new troubles as he now worried whether he would be able to travel Asia again because of his responsibility to the animals.

East Hill Farm, like most places Allen settled for

more than a few weeks, was decorated with countless trinkets he'd picked up during his world-wanderings. Surrounded by all these memories of far-flung locations, he flitted between a desire to stay put and the familiar urge to head back out on the road again. He told Snyder, "I've travelled so much so hard . . . I want to stay here in one place as long as I can . . . find my own body rhythm outside of airplane drone in my skull." Yet later he changed his mind, saying "I think I need to go around the world again" and explaining that he now wanted to see Australia, Borobudur, Polynesia, Persia, and even return to India. In his journals, he flitted back and forth between the desire to stay put and the urge to go back to Asia. The only thing he didn't want to do was keep on travelling around America, giving poetry readings, but he had little choice, and so he travelled continually to pay his bills and support the various causes that attracted his sympathy.

By November, 1968, Allen's exhausting schedule had taken its toll on his health, and when he was involved in a car crash he ended up with a broken hip that forced him to slow down for a while. The following year he missed the event of the decade at Woodstock, even though it was only eighty miles from his home at Cherry Valley. He was still tired and reluctant to travel unnecessarily, and told his father that he would soon retire from poetry readings. He wanted to go abroad and escape his American obligations, but as Bill Morgan notes, travel had become a "nuisance" because "Every time Allen left the country he was under continual surveillance."[52] He was rigorously searched just crossing the border into Canada, and again on the way back. It happened nearly every time he left the country, and it appeared to be getting worse as sometimes he was not only interrogated, but searched and stripped. Indeed, his anti-war protests had once again drawn attention from above, and according to his F.B.I. files, by the late sixties and early seventies he was very much on their radar once again.

That same month, Allen's next collection of poems was released through City Lights. As with *Howl and Other Poems* (1956), *Kaddish and Other Poems* (1961), and *Reality Sandwiches* (1963), *Planet News* was another collection of poems written during, or inspired by, his travels. There are poems written on boats ("Sunset S.S. Azemour"), planes ("Kral Majales"), and trains ("The Change: Kyoto-Tokyo Express"). There are poems composed in Israel ("Galilee Shore"), Greece ("Seabattle of Salamis Took Place off Perama"), India ("Describe: The Rain on Dasaswamedh Ghat"), Czechoslovakia ("Big Beat"), Poland ("Café in Warsaw), and elsewhere. Even the poems written back in the U.S. are often composed on the road or allude to his travels. It was, as the title suggests, a book concerning the whole planet. Many reviewers admired his juxtaposition of personal and planetary details, or the introspective mixed with the international, but one reviewer for the *New York Review of Books* failed to appreciate this and Ginsberg was upset, as Gordon Ball recalls, that his book "was denounced for being too planetary or personally detailed".[53] Allen's own description of this collection puts a special emphasis on the importance of travel, citing various locations and journeys as integral to the composition of this collection:

> Planet News collecting seven years' Poesy scribed to 1967 begins with electronic politics disassociation & messianic rhapsody TV Baby in New York, continues picaresque around the globe, elan perceptions notated at Mediterranean, Galilee & Ganges till next breakthrough, comedown Poem at heart & soul last days in Asia The Change 1963; tenement doldrums & police-state paranoia in Manhattan then half year behind Socialist Curtain climaxed as Kral Majales May King Prague 1965, same years' erotic gregariousness writ as Who Be Kind To for International Poetry Incarnation Albert Hall London; next trip West Coast thru center America Midwest Wichita Vortex Sutra . . . at last across Atlantic Wales Visitation . . .

Ginsberg's travels from this point on were less solitary adventures into the unknown and more comfortable, organised trips with friends, family, or his assistants. In 1968, he was able to travel a little with his family. First, he took a trip back to Mexico with his brother Eugene and his wife and children. There were eight of them crammed into Allen's little V.W. bus, and at the border Allen was detained for three hours as they told him, "We don't let hippies and communists and

Jews in."[54] Fortunately, he was able to gain permission to enter the country without, as they originally wanted, cutting off his hair and beard. After two weeks showing them around Mexico, he met his father in San Francisco and acted as tour guide there, before heading back home to Cherry Valley to complete a staggering 9,000 mile round-trip in his trusty van. Both Mexico and San Francisco were hugely important parts of Allen's literary life, and it is significant that he chose to share them at this point with his family.

In 1970, he visited Haiti for a week with his father, and then visited Antigua, Bermuda, and the Virgin Islands with his attorney, William Kunstler. The following year, he went to Puerto Rico with Lucien Carr, who often travelled there. Allen later wrote "Vomit Express" with Bob Dylan about the trip. The phrase "Vomit Express" had been coined by Carr, and referred to the number of poor people taking advantage of cheap tickets to fly for the first time and then getting sick on the plane.

In 1971, with Gordon Ball now acting as his road manager to take care of logistics, Allen returned to India. The trip was paid for by Keith Richards and he was accompanied by the poet, John Giorno. He visited the refugee camps near Calcutta, then saw Benares again, and returned to his favourite ghats. As with so many of his later travels, he made great efforts to meet up with old friends. The refugee camps were set up for people escaping the Bangladesh genocide, and after visiting Allen wrote one of his greatest poems, "September on Jessore Road":

Millions of babies watching the skies
Bellies swollen, with big round eyes
On Jessore Road-long bamboo huts
Noplace to shit but sand channel ruts

Millions of fathers in rain
Millions of mothers in pain
Millions of brothers in woe
Millions of sisters nowhere to go[55]

By the early seventies, one of Allen's primary interests was ecology and he was becoming increasingly aware of the damage humans were doing to their environment. In 1971, he wrote a letter from a plane that speculated that the "Airplane Age" "can't last too long"[56] and the following year he expressed guilt over his extensive world travels, as he had been "flying around exhausting gas"[57]. Indeed, he was never off the road for very long. For one reason or another, he would soon end up flying or driving to somewhere far away, and living in hotels for long periods of time.

Allen's next trip came in 1972, when he and Lawrence Ferlinghetti travelled together to Australia. On the way, they stopped off for a day in Hawaii and then a week in Fiji, where Allen went snorkelling on the Sigatoka coral reef. Although it was a short visit, Fiji inspired Ginsberg to write several songs. In Australia, they travelled from Adelaide to Melbourne and then Sydney, before visiting Ayers Rock (now more commonly referred to by its original name, Uluru) in the centre of the country, and Arnhem Land in the north. As always, Allen managed to cram in as much sightseeing as possible, but also took the opportunity to mix with the locals and learn about the culture of the place. In particular, he was interested in the aboriginal people, whom he soon realised had an even worse situation than the Native Americans back in the U.S. He was fascinated by their culture and tried learning some of their music and poetry. At the Adelaide Festival of the Arts, he invited some aboriginal people on stage with him, which enraged the white audience. Allen commented that he would even have considered moving to Australia except that the country's history made for some "tough white karma" of which he wanted no part.[58] While Allen remained in Australia, by late March Ferlinghetti ventured over to New Zealand, and warned Allen away. He said it was exactly like California and the indigenous culture had long since died off.

Back in the U.S., Allen continued to give public readings of his work for money. Although he was at times keen to retire from such a life, he was also unable to stop giving his money away. A huge amount of what he earned was funnelled into various charitable causes, and so he was perpetually broke. Some of it did go on his own personal interests, although often these overlapped with the public good, or with the needs of his friends and fellow artists. By 1974, he was earning an impressive $1,000 per day for reading his poetry. Bob Rosenthal noted that:

> Allen has an aptitude for making money;
> offers just come in. However, Allen doesn't
> accumulate money; he lives from hand to
> many mouths.[59]

In June, 1973, Allen flew back to Europe, first stopping off in the Netherlands for a poetry festival. Here, he visited Rotterdam and Delft, before moving on to explore the U.K. once again. He found England had changed a great deal since the Swinging Sixties. For one thing, it was far more expensive than it used to be. Although he was in town for a big poetry conference, and also did some TV and radio work, he was stuck in a "fleabag room" for his stay.[60] He observed that the economic conditions had affected everything, including poetry and clothing, and that London was no longer the bright and vivacious place it used to be. He also spent some time with Burroughs, who was in his final year of self-imposed exile from the United States. After that, he ventured north of the border to Scotland, where he attended a reading in Glasgow, met with the poet, Scott Eden, and visited Iona Abbey. His tour lasted two months.

Due to poor health and a lack of cash, Allen did very little travel for the next two years. However, in 1976 he was able to return to Europe on two separate trips. The first took him to Belgium and France, and the second to France and Germany. As with most of these later travels, he was not alone, and in France he visited Gregory Corso. In Germany, Allen travelled with Burroughs to Berlin. "I've never been there," he excitedly told Gary

Snyder.[61] In fact, Allen had wanted to visit Berlin with Burroughs about twenty years earlier, when they were living at the Beat Hotel.

In the coming years, Allen made numerous trips to Europe, sometimes touring for months at a time.* He saw almost every country on the continent and most of the major cities. Now, however, his tours were mostly managed and at every stop he was scheduled to give a reading of his poetry, and often he would consult with publishers and translators about versions of his work being released in those countries. By 1979, Bob Rosenthal was organizing Allen's trips, and one European tour alone took a solid three months of planning.[62] He travelled with assistants and accompanying musicians, and often acted as a tour guide now that he had several decades of experience touring Europe. He never tired of seeing the sights himself, always stopping off at museums and other places of interest.

Rosenthal commented on the nature of his trips at this point:

> Allen is often being offered extravagant vacations. He has been offered mountain escapes in Hawaii, trips to the hanging gardens in Turkey and spa breaks in Italy. Allen doesn't go on vacation just for

---

* From this point onwards, due to Allen's many short travels or repeat visits to the same places, I will skip over some tours in favour of more important travel experiences. A full list of places Allen visited can be found at the end of this book.

relaxation. He goes to visit the close friends that live there. For down time and freedom from public scrutiny, he stays home—in the Lower East Side.[63]

In 1980, he went on an epic tour of Eastern Europe, finally getting to see Hungary. He had wanted to go there in 1965, but his troubles in Czechoslovakia had prevented him from doing so. Over two long months, he thoroughly explored Yugoslavia and the Balkans, as well as some central European countries. "Every country in Europe is a world of own," he remarked.[64] On this trip, he wrote the poems "Birdbrain" and "Eroica." As with all his travels in the eighties, he was beset by health problems, but these didn't stop him from taking in all the views and soaking up all of the history of each place he managed to visit.

Ginsberg's next important journey came in 1982, when he visited Nicaragua. On 21st January, he travelled to Managua to attend the Rubén Darío poetry festival. Allen was met at the airport by the president, Daniel Ortega, who was not only a solider, but also a poet. In fact, it seemed to Allen that everyone had an interest in poetry. Everywhere he went, people cared about poetry and he was even able to read his work to soldiers during a visit to Lago de Nicaragua. He very much enjoyed his visit, and together with fellow poets Yevtushenko and Ernesto Cardenal he wrote the "Declaration of Three" statement, which asked for the U.S. and U.S.S.R. to cease their interventionist policies, which were destroying lives in countries like Nicaragua.

Allen continued to tour Europe frequently, and the following year he finally made it to Scandinavia. During a tour of a dozen European nations, Allen travelled through Denmark, Sweden, Finland, and Norway, before moving on to Germany. Together with Orlovsky and Steven Taylor, he took a train from Amsterdam to Copenhagen, and spent almost two weeks giving readings throughout the country, before moving on to Sweden. Next, in Finland, he stayed with Beat scholar, Ann Charters, who had written a book on Kerouac a decade earlier. Everywhere they went, they tried to stay with locals because they were on such a tight budget. Allen had a piece of paper on which he kept meticulous notes on expenditure, and as people were more than happy to take him in, he was able to save considerably by relying on the kindness of others. In Denmark, though, Gregory Stephenson offered to buy them lunch, and Allen protested: "We have money; we're just cheap."[65]

In descriptions of Allen's earlier, perhaps more significant, travels, I explained the importance of art to Allen. Wherever he went, he sought out museums and galleries, to the point that his travels were often dictated by what towns had works by major artists. This never changed, and in his later years he just pushed further, finding works he'd never seen before, or hadn't seen in a long time. He hunted down manuscripts by Blake when visiting England, and here in Scandinavia he hunted down important paintings. Stephenson recalls Allen taking a break from his packed schedule to meander through the National Gallery. In stark contrast with the hectic reading schedule and errands to acquire visas for Sweden, "Allen is unhurried, focused, engaged and attentive in regarding the paintings."[66] He had already read up on local artists such as Nicolai Abildgaard and Emil Nolde, and was delighted to find works by Bruegel, Rembrandt, and Rubens. Although he was now very much an old man and his travels were very different to those undertaken in his youth, Allen maintained a similar attitude in some ways.

This trip was the last time Allen travelled with Peter Orlovsky, who suffered a massive breakdown while in Amsterdam, prior to the Scandinavian leg of the tour. Everywhere he went he either amused or appalled people with his bizarre and often shocking antics. He had proven extremely difficult to handle, and although Allen was accustomed to his problems, others, including Steven Taylor, refused to put up with it anymore. For the next decade, Peter would stay at home while Allen continued touring.

China

It may seem strange that it was only in 1984 that Allen Ginsberg finally managed to travel to China. He had shown an interest in China since he was a boy, and that had only grown through his life until Chinese art and culture became somewhat of an obsession in 1953, when he began studying Asian paintings in New York. He often travelled to exotic places and compared them to what he thought China was like, and everywhere he went he sought out Chinese food and paid attention to the news coming out from China. He was quite well-versed in Chinese literature, and admired poets who were heavily influenced by Chinese poetry, including Ezra Pound, and his friends, Gary Snyder and Kenneth Rexroth. Ginsberg had mentioned an interest in visiting China countless times throughout his life, but had failed to visit. Of course, it was not an easy country to explore after Mao Zedong came to power in 1949, and few westerners had the opportunity.

In 1982, Ginsberg and Snyder had welcomed Chinese writers from the Peking Writers' Union to America, and in 1984 the favour was returned. A delegation of famous American writers travelled to Beijing for a short, boring conference in China's capital. They were taken to all the major cultural attractions, including the Great Wall and the Forbidden City. China, he said, is "clean and safe and vast and comfortable" like a "clean crowded India."[67] Allen was not impressed by the conference, but enjoyed meeting the other writers and exploring this fascinating, ancient city. "More than anything he loved being a tourist and seeing new places," Bill Morgan remarked, when referring to Allen's visit to China.[68]

The writers were ferried around by chaperones, but Ginsberg also sought advice from Gary Snyder, who could speak Chinese. As he had done in India, he helped explain and interpret everything for Allen. For a month, they saw Beijing, then travelled to the ancient capital of Xi'an, then the modern metropolis of Shanghai and nearby Suzhou, a peaceful town of gardens and waterways, as well as the Han Shan Temple, Hangzhou, and then Guangzhou in the south of the country. With Gary's help, Allen was able to ask probing questions about sex and politics, which were topics that his guides would not have encouraged. He found that most Chinese students were incredibly naïve about sex, denying even that homosexuality existed (gay sex was in fact illegal at that time). In regard to politics, people seemed mostly happy with their government, although they all agreed that the Cultural Revolution had been a tremendous mistake. He was careful to avoid criticising the Chinese government or asking questions that were too probing, but he still managed to delve deep into what people really thought, and wrote a fascinating essay on his findings, simply titled, "China Trip."

The group arrived in China on 14th October and left on 6th November, but Allen stayed behind, having sought permission to stay in China for a few more months. He had asked to teach at some universities and this was approved, so after bidding farewell to his fellow writers, he continued on his own through the vast Middle Kingdom. From Guangzhou, he flew to Chongqing and then took a riverboat to Wuhan for a three-day cruise through the famous Three Gorges. Everywhere he went he was accompanied by guides, except for this boat trip, and so it was a particular highlight of his time in China. When he saw some western hippie travellers in fourth class, he envied their position. It reminded him of his own experiences as an anonymous young man venturing through strange countries.

From Wuhan, Allen flew to Beijing for a few days' teaching, and then spent a further month and a half working at different institutions throughout China. Much of his time there was spent in Baoding, a little under a hundred miles southwest of the capital. However, he spent most of the time in bed with bronchitis. Everywhere he went in China, the pollution was horrendous and caused him to suffer all sorts of ailments. He had to give up smoking because his lungs were so badly affected. When he did get out and explore, he found Baoding was the "real China" rather than the tourist sites he'd visited elsewhere, as there was "no façade created for tourists,"[69] and he was able to communicate with the people he met. He spoke with Christians and Muslims, but was saddened to see that most religion had been wiped out since the implementation of communist rule. He managed to communicate well, as long as it was on an individual level: "one to one they talk frankly—but three's a crowd!!"[70] In a later essay, he emphasised this, saying that people would even go as far as to criticise Mao Zedong in private, but with any other Chinese nearby they would become fearful and say nothing.

At the beginning of December, he took the train south to Shanghai, where he arrived sick and miserable. While bed-ridden for a week, he wrote one of his most beautiful poems, "Reading Bai Juyi," which begins:

> I'm a traveler in a strange country
> China and I've been to many cities
> Now I'm back in Shanghai, days

under warm covers in a room with electric
heat—
a rare commodity in this country —
hundreds of millions shiver in the north[71]

The poem muses on Allen's Chinese poetic
influence, Bai Juyi, as well as the country's present
political situation and his experiences there. The final
section, "Part VII," is an imitation of Bai Juyi's "A
Night in Xingyang,"* that explores Allen's own life. Interestingly, writing from China, he reflects on being a
young boy lying on his parents' "Chinese rug" in their
Paterson home, "daydreaming" about going out to
visit the world, which he had now, at age fifty-eight,
seen. In a later reading of this poem, he puts a heavy
emphasis on the first word, "I," as though directly
answering Bai's own experiences. Ginsberg mentions in
his introduction to the reading that Bai was well-travelled in China, and Allen seems to be completing a conversation with him, replying with his own mirrored
experience. Although not at all well-known, the poem
is in my mind one of Ginsberg's finest works.

In Shanghai, he spent a week in bed, and then went
out to explore further, before moving on to Nanjing,
another old capital not far to the west. Here he saw

---

* Although this is what Ginsberg claimed Bai's poem was called, there is
no English translation that I can find with the same name. Arthur Waley
wrote several translations, including "Stopping the Night at Rong-yang"
and "Stopping the Night at Jung-yang." A translation of the original
poem, as well as an essay on Ginsberg's interpretation, are included in the
appendix.

the Ming tombs and found that some monks were allowed to continue practicing Buddhism, albeit under strict government supervision. Finally, he visited the vast western provinces of Sichuan and Yunnan, before flying back home to the U.S. at the very end of the year.

Throughout his time in China, Ginsberg wrote much poetry inspired by what he saw. However, China had been an inspiration for him long before he ever set foot in the country. A poem he wrote in Beijing during the conference in October explains all the reasons why he became a poet, and more than a few refer explicitly to China, including the line:

> I write poetry because Pound pointed young Western poets to look at Chinese writing word pictures.[72]

Final Journeys

In 1985, Allen ventured back behind the Iron Curtain, visiting Russia, Lithuania, Georgia, and Byelorussia (now known as Belarus). Once again, he was participating in a delegation of American writers travelling to a communist country, and again he requested permission to stay and travel alone after the official visit had ended. However, he was only granted a short additional stay. During his time in the Soviet Union, while closely watched by his chaperones, he managed to see the cities of Vilnius, Minsk, and Tbilisi, as well as revisiting Moscow and St. Petersburg. His travelling buddy for the trip was playwright Arthur Miller, with whom he did extensive sightseeing. After Miller left, Ginsberg continued alone for two weeks, seeing museums and other places of interest.

It had been twenty years since Allen last visited the Soviet Union, but he noted that little had changed since then. The following year, he returned to Nicaragua and was equally disappointed. He had been impressed on his first visit, but it turned out the Sandinistas had not been the progressive leaders he hoped, and the country was in a mess. In response to American meddling, the government had become more repressive in an attempt to stamp out any dissent. He was bitterly disappointed to see socialism failing in yet another country.

Soon after, Ginsberg flew to Budapest, in Hungary, another country suffering under communism, for a relaxing week alone in the ancient city divided by the Danube River. His hotel room gave him a wonderful view of the historic skyline, and when he went out he was treated as a rock star because his poetry had been made into rock anthems by the Hobo Blues Band. Allen even performed with them on stage in a huge amphi-theatre. Next, he flew to Yugoslavia, another socialist republic. First, he arrived at Struga, in Macedonia, on the border with Albania, where he received a Golden Wreath at the Struga Poetry Evenings literary festival. It was the country's most prestigious literary award, and at the ceremony, held by Lake Ohrid, he even met the Macedonian president. Later, he also visited Skopje and Closter, before moving on to Zagreb in Croatia and Belgrade in Serbia. He finished up his tour of socialist nations with a train ride to Krakow and Warsaw in

Poland.

Back in the U.S., Allen was told by a doctor to stop travelling because of his bad health. This time it was an arrhythmia, or an irregular heartbeat. Although he didn't plan on stopping, he did decline a journey through Tibet with Snyder—something Ginsberg had always wanted to do. It was the trip of a lifetime, the culmination of decades of growing interest in Tibetan Buddhism. When he developed bronchitis once again, any chance of a trip to Tibet faded away.

In 1988, Ginsberg travelled with the photographer Robert Frank to Israel, which he hadn't visited since 1961. Despite being an outspoken critic of Israel's persecution of the Palestinian people, he was invited to give readings in Haifa and Jerusalem. Allen attended a peace rally and visited the Wailing Wall, which he hadn't been able to see on his first visit. He also managed to sneak into neighbouring Palestine for several days, where he spoke to children who collected the scrap metal left over from bombs that had been dropped—bombs that had been made in the U.S. He stuck around in Tel Aviv for three weeks to teach with Frank at the Camera Obscura School of Art. Ginsberg's class was called "Photographic Poetics."

In October, he returned to Japan, and in 1990 he returned to Prague in what was now the Czech Republic. The Berlin Wall had fallen and Eastern Europe was finally freeing itself from decades of Soviet-imposed horror. The new Czech president was Václav Havel, who had met Allen at the May Day festival in 1965 and then again in the café where Allen most likely lost his notebook. Havel promised to help Allen get it back, but it was never found. As well as hanging out at a pub with the president, Allen managed to visit České Budějovice, Southern Bohemia, and the ancient Boubín Forest, the largest indigenous forest in Central Europe.

He continued to tour Europe in the early nineties and in 1990 made it to Turkey, which had eluded him on previous travels in the region. In the summer, he visited South Korea, which he mostly found boring. He said he only visited it because it was a new country—the sixty-third country he'd been to—but still made the effort to travel around and see much of what it had to offer.

In late 1992, he embarked upon his last long journey—an epic reading tour lasting four months and taking him through a dozen countries. Starting in Vienna, Austria, he voyaged through Hungary, Yugoslavia, Germany, Poland, England, Ireland, Norway, Czech Republic, Spain, Greece, and Morocco. He had never visited the Emerald Isle on any of his many trips to the U.K., and so when he finally got to Ireland—both Northern Ireland and the Republic of Ireland—he had a long list of places to see. He took the opportunity to see his favourite painting, Brueghel's *Tower of Babel*, one last time and visited old friends—Lucian Carr in Barcelona, Alan Ansen in Athens, and Paul Bowles in Tangier. He hadn't been back to Tangier since 1961, and he made time to go visit his old room at the Hotel Muniria, where the tiled balcony had become cracked and the garden overgrown. "I cried to think how innocently happy we were together that trip to

Europe," he told Peter.[73] Life moved along a lot faster now, and instead of donkeys there were cars in the streets.

By 1994, Allen was still travelling around Europe regularly and making plans to visit Indonesia, but more than ever his health failed him. By now he had hepatitis A, B, and C, as well as diabetes and congestive heart failure, for which he had to wear a nitroglycerin path. "My heart's still pumping but especially in travel I get out of breath easily, feel older and less energetic," he explained to Gary Snyder, finally giving up on the idea of ever travelling to Tibet.[74] The following year was much the same, and he took some more time out of his reading schedule to relax by the Mediterranean. He was struggling, but never lost his enthusiasm for being a tourist: "Tired but sightseeing I've got energy for one castle a day and lots of naps."[75]

Yet he was ultimately reluctant to slow down. Bob Rosenthal tried to help Allen reduce his reading schedule, sometimes without telling him, but Allen would not give up his readings entirely. They meant the world to him, even if he collapsed "into an exhausted heap" after each one.[76] Rosenthal urged him to focus on his work at Brooklyn College rather than persist in flying about the world for poetry readings:

> Teaching at Brooklyn College is a concession to his slowing down. When he travels to read poetry, he enjoys the open faces of young people with their ears cocked for his voice. At Brooklyn College,

> he holds the class in rapt attention without
> the hassle of flying. [77]

After being suddenly and unexpectedly diagnosed with cancer, Allen Ginsberg died on 5th April, 1997. He had planned to retire from teaching in May of that year, so that he would "be able to travel abroad more freely if health permits."[78] He even planned to travel to Italy with Orlovsky, which would have been their first trip together in almost fifteen years, but as the end drew near, it too was cancelled. His last full poem was "Things I'll Not Do," which he wrote in the days before his death. Beginning, "Never go to Bulgaria, had a booklet & invitation", it is essentially a list of places he still wanted to see (Albania, Tibet, Egypt, Syria, Afghanistan), or important places he wanted to return to (India, China, Morocco), but which, as he says in the final line, he would never get to visit "except in an urn of ashes."

Although his final poem lamented those remaining places he would never have the chance to visit, Ginsberg had—in the fifty years since his first foreign trip in 1947—managed to see an astonishing sixty-six countries. His travels had made him a citizen of the world. He felt as comfortable in an Indian slum, a Cambodian jungle, or a Mexican plantation, as he did back in the country of his birth. Wherever he went, he felt at home among the local people because he was one of them. In a 1978 interview, he was asked whether, "in your travels and in the sense that you really encompass most of the world" he had become "the persona that Whitman was projecting". Allen replied in the affirmative:

> Well, I was working consciously to do some of that, but it was more like the natural thing, like we've got airplanes now so it is inevitable. I was working consciously out of the Whitmanic tradition, once I read him, thinking, now what did he do that needs to be fulfilled . . .[79]

Yes, he enjoyed playing the role of the tourist, guidebook and camera in hand, but he was never the detached observer learning purely through books and museums. He always spoke with the local people and learned from them. He was a man of the world, viewing national borders, religious beliefs, and racial distinctions as barriers to peace and love between people. In 1970, he wrote to his father:

> As I would not see myself as Black if I were black, I don't see myself as a Jew as I am a Jew & so don't identify with Nation of Jews anymore than I would of Nation of America or Russia. Down with all nations they are enemies of mankind! And nationalism is disease.[80]

Indeed, Allen Ginsberg was truly a World Citizen.

Notes

Bibliography

A special thank you to the Allen Ginsberg Project, which hosts invaluable archival material at http://ginsbergblog.blogspot.com/ and http://allenginsberg.org/.

Ball, Gordon, *East Hill Farm* (Counterpoint: Berkeley, 2011)

Burroughs, William, and Ginsberg, Allen, *The Yagé Letters Redux* (City Lights: San Francisco, 2006)

Ewing, E. Thomas and Hicks, David (eds), *Education & The Great Depression: Lessons from a Global History* (Peter Lang: New York, 2006)

Ginsberg, Allen, *Collected Poems 1947-1997* (Penguin: London, 2009)

Ginsberg, Allen, *Selected Poems 1947-1995* (HarperCollins: New York, 2001)

Ginsberg, Allen, *Indian Journals* (Grove Press: New York, 1996)

Ginsberg, Allen, and Morgan, Bill (ed) *Wait Til I'm Dead: Uncollected Poems* (Grove: New York, 2016)

Ginsberg, Allen, and Ball, Gordon (ed), *Journals: Early Fifties Early Sixties* (Grove Press: New York, 1977)

Ginsberg, Allen, and Morgan, Bill (ed), *Deliberate Prose: Selected Essays 1952-1995* (Harper Perennial, 2001)

Ginsberg, Allen, and Schumacher, Michael (ed), *Iron Curtain Journals: January-May 1965* (University of Minnesota Press: Minneapolis, 2018) (uncorrected pre-publication copy)

Kipling, Rudyard, *Kim*

Lardas, John, *The Bop Apocalypse: The Religious Visions of Kerouac, Ginsberg, and Burroughs* (University of Illinois: 2001)

Liebermann-Plimpton, Juanita, and Morgan, Bill (eds), *The Book of Martyrdom and Artifice* (Da Capo, 2006)

Miles, Barry, *Ginsberg: A Biography* (Virgin: London, 2000)

Miles, Barry, *In the Sixties* (Rocket 88, London, 2018)

Miles, Barry, *The Beat Hotel: Ginsberg, Burroughs, and Corso in Paris, 1957–63* (Grove Press: New York, 2000)

Moore, Dave (ed), *Neal Cassady: Collected letters 1944–1967* (Penguin: New York, 2004)

Morgan, Bill, and Stanford, David (eds), *Jack Kerouac and Allen Ginsberg: The Letters* (Viking: New York, 2010)

Morgan, Bill, *Best Minds of My Generation: A Literary History of the Beats* (Grove Press: 2017)

Morgan, Bill (ed), *The Letters of Allen Ginsberg* (Da Dapo: Philadelphia, 2008)

Morgan, Bill, *The Beats Aboard: A Global Guide to the Beat Generation* (City Lights, San Francisco, 2015)

Morgan, Bill, *I Celebrate Myself: The Somewhat Private Life of Allen Ginsberg* (Viking: New York, 2006)

Morgan, Bill (ed), *The Selected Letters of Allen Ginsberg and Gary Snyder* (Counterpoint: Berkeley, 2009)

Morgan, Bill (ed), *I Greet You at the Beginning of a Great Career: The Selected Correspondence of Lawrence Ferlinghetti and Allen Ginsberg, 1955–1997* (City Lights: San Francisco, 2015)

Morgan, Bill (ed), *An Accidental Autobiography: The Selected Letters of Gregory Corso* (New Directions: 2003)

Raskin, Jonah, *American Scream: Allen Ginsberg's Howl and the Making of the Beat Generation* (University of California Press: Berkeley, 2005)

Rosenthal, Bob, *Straight Around Allen* (Beatdom Books: St. Andrews, 2018)

Schumacher, Michael, (ed), *The Essential Ginsberg* (HarperCollins: New York, 2015)

Schumacher, Michael (ed), *Family Business: Selected Letters*

Between a Father and a Son: Allen and Louis Ginsberg
(Bloomsbury: London, 2001)

Schumacher, Michael (ed), *First Thought: Conversations with Allen Ginsberg* (University of Minnesota Press: Minneapolis, 2017)

Trigilio, Tony, *Allen Ginsberg's Buddhist Poetics* (Southern Illinois University Press: Carbondale, 2007)

Tytell, John, *Beat Transnationalism*, (Beatdom: St. Andrews, 2017)

Other Sources:
FBI File via FOI at https://vault.fbi.gov/irwin-allen-ginsberg

Notes on Part 1

1 David Hicks, Education & The Great Depression, p.24
2 Bill Morgan, I Celebrate Myself, p.31
3 http://forward.com/culture/11112/portrait-of-the-artist-as-a-nice-jewish-boy-00111/
4 Allen Ginsberg, The Book of Martyrdom and Artifice, p.14
5 Martyrdom and Artifice, p.11
6 I Celebrate Myself, p.41
7 First thought, p.19
8 I Celebrate Myself, p.36
9 Ginsberg, Allen, The Letters of Allen Ginsberg, p.7
10 Book of Martyrdom and Artifice, p.56
11 Book of Martyrdom and Artifice, p.63
12 Book of Martyrdom and Artifice, p.401
13 The Letters of Allen Ginsberg, p.394
14 Book of Martyrdom and Artifice, p.407
15 Book of Martyrdom and Artifice, p.409
16 Book of Martyrdom and Artifice, p.92
17 Book of Martyrdom and Artifice, p.123
18 Ginsberg, Allen, Family Business, p59
19 Jack Kerouac and Allen Ginsberg: The Letters, p.9

20 Book of Martyrdom and Artifice, p.126
21 Jack Kerouac and Allen Ginsberg: The Letters p.13
22 Book of Martyrdom and Artifice, p,126
23 Book of Martyrdom and Artifice, p.128
24 Book of Martyrdom and Artifice p.423
25 Book of Martyrdom and Artifice p.130
26 ibid
27 http://ginsbergblog.blogspot.com/2012/01/louis-allen-1975-naropa-class.html
28 http://allenginsberg.org/2016/11/fulke-greville-hart-cranes-atlantis/
29 Book of Martyrdom and Artifice, p.132
30 Book of Martyrdom and Artifice p.136
31 Book of Martyrdom and Artifice p.433
32 Book of Martyrdom and Artifice p.434
33 Book of Martyrdom and Artifice p.441
34 Book of Martyrdom and Artifice p.213
35 Moore, Dave, Neal Cassady: Collected letters 1944-1967, p.47
36 Book of Martyrdom and Artifice, p. 211
37 Book of Martyrdom and Artifice, p.213
38 I Celebrate Myself, p.88
39 Book of Martyrdom and Artifice, p.213
40 Miles, Barry, Ginsberg: A Biography, p.89
41 Family Business, p.15
42 ibid
43 Neal Cassady: Collected Letters, p.56
44 Ginsberg, Allen, Journals: Early Fifties Early Sixties, p.19
45 Family Business, p.16-17
46 Family Business p.15
47 I Celebrate Myself, p.96
48 Book of Martyrdom and Artifice, p.213
49 Book of Martyrdom and Artifice, p.470
50 The Letters of Allen Ginsberg, p.20
51 Book of Martyrdom and Artifice, p.232-233
52 Book of Martyrdom and Artifice, p.228
53 ibid

54 ibid
55 Jack Kerouac and Allen Ginsberg: The Letters, p.115
56 Book of Martyrdom and Artifice, p.378
57 Book of Martyrdom and Artifice, p.231
58 Ginsberg: A Biography, p.102-103
59 Qtd in Ginsberg: A Biography, p.103
60 Book of Martyrdom and Artifice, p.257
61 ibid
62 Book of Martyrdom and Artifice, p.496
63 Jack Kerouac and Allen Ginsberg: The Letters, p.171
64 Bob Rosenthal, Straight Around Allen, p.70

Notes on Part 2
1 The Book of Martyrdom and Artifice, p.381
2 Jack Kerouac and Allen Ginsberg: The Letters, p.152
3 Jack Kerouac and Allen Ginsberg: The Letters, p.170
4 Ginsberg: A Biography, 144
5 Journals: Early Fifties Early Sixties, xvii
6 Qtd in I Celebrate Myself, p.157
7 Qtd in I Celebrate Myself, p.149
8 I Celebrate Myself, p.152
9 Qtd in Allen Ginsberg: A Biography, p.153
10 Family Business, p.210
11 The Letters of Allen Ginsberg, p.90
12 Journals: Early Fifties Early Sixties, p.38
13 ibid
14 The Letters of Allen Ginsberg, p.91
15 Morgan, Bill, Best Minds of My Generation: A Literary History of the Beats, ebook – no page number
16 Ginsberg, Allen, Collected Poems, p.100
17 http://ginsbergblog.blogspot.com/2011/08/spiritual-po-etics-5.html
18 The Letters of Allen Ginsberg, p.91..
19 Journals: Early Fifties Early Sixties, p.29
20 The Letters of Allen Ginsberg p.91
21 Journals: Early Fifties Early Sixties, p.31
22 Journals: Early Fifties Early Sixties, p.33

23 Journals: Early Fifties Early Sixties, p.38
24 The Letters of Allen Ginsberg, p.92
25 The Letters of Allen Ginsberg, p.92
26 Journals: Early Fifties Early Sixties, p.40
27 Journals: Early Fifties Early Sixties, p.40
28 Journals: Early Fifties Early Sixties, p.41
29 Ginsberg: A Biography, p.156
30 Best Minds of My Generation: A Literary History of the Beats, ebook – no page number
31 Journals: Early Fifties Early Sixties, p.42
32 Jack Kerouac and Allen Ginsberg: The Letters, p.210
33 Jack Kerouac and Allen Ginsberg: The Letters, p.209
34 Selected Poems, p.30
35 https://allenginsberg.org/2012/02/green-valentine/
36 Ginsberg: A Biography, p.157
37 Jack Kerouac and Allen Ginsberg: The Letters, p.214
38 Jack Kerouac and Allen Ginsberg: The Letters, p.215
39 Jack Kerouac and Allen Ginsberg: The Letters, p.216
40 Qtd in Ginsberg: A Biography, p.160
41 Jack Kerouac and Allen Ginsberg: The Letters, p.216
42 Journals: Early Fifties Early Sixties, p.64
43 Journals: Early Fifties Early Sixties, p.66
44 Journals: Early Fifties Early Sixties, p.69
45 Jack Kerouac and Allen Ginsberg: The Letters, p.215
46 Raskin, Jonah, American Scream: Allen Ginsberg's Howl and the Making of the Beat Generation, p.119
47 Best Minds of My Generation, Kindle – no page number
48 ibid
49 Tytell, John, Beat Transnationalism, p.30
50 Beat Transnationalism, p.120
51 The Letters of Allen Ginsberg, p.214
52 American Scream, p. 118
53 Schumacher, Michael (ed), Essential Ginsberg, p.148
54 Essential Ginsberg, p.xiv
55 ibid
56 Journals: Early Fifties Early Sixties, p.55
57 Jack Kerouac and Allen Ginsberg: The Letters, p.244

58 The Letters of Allen Ginsberg, p.93
59 Jack Kerouac and Allen Ginsberg: The Letters, p.232
60 Jack Kerouac and Allen Ginsberg: The Letters, p.263
61 Morgan, Bill (ed), The Selected Letters of Allen Ginsberg and Gary Snyder, p.vii
62 Letters of Allen Ginsberg and Gary Snyder, p.10
63 The Letters of Allen Ginsberg, p.120
64 Letters of Allen Ginsberg and Gary Snyder, p.10
65 Jack Kerouac and Allen Ginsberg: The Letters, p,334
66 Letters of Allen Ginsberg and Gary Snyder, p.13
67 Qtd in I Celebrate Myself, p.232
68 Ginsberg: A Biography, p.220
69 Jack Kerouac and Allen Ginsberg: The Letters, p.341
70 Letters of Allen Ginsberg and Gary Snyder,p.20
71 The Letters of Allen Ginsberg, p.133
72 Jack Kerouac and Allen Ginsberg: The Letters,p.210
73 The Letters of Allen Ginsberg, p.135
74 ibid
75 Letters of Allen Ginsberg and Gary Snyder, p.20
76 The Letters of Allen Ginsberg, p.138
77 The Letters of Allen Ginsberg, p 136
78 I Celebrate Myself, p.247
79 Ginsberg: A Biography, p.223
80 Jean Genet, The Thief's Journal, p.12
81 Jack Kerouac and Allen Ginsberg: The Letters, p.341
82 The Letters of Allen Ginsberg, p.141
83 Ginsberg: A Biography, p. 224
84 Morgan, Bill (ed), I Greet You at the Beginning of a Great Career: The Selected Correspondence of Lawrence Ferling-hetti and Allen Ginsberg, 1955-1997, p.35
85 Family Business, p.64
86 I Greet You at the Beginning of a Great Career, p.36
87 Family Business, p.65
88 Qtd in Ginsberg: A Biography, p.226
89 ibid
90 Family Business, p.66
91 The Letters of Allen Ginsberg, p.192

92 Family Biz p.69
93 Letters of Allen Ginsberg and Gary Snyder, p.21
94 Family Business, p.69
95 Iron Curtain Journals, p.274
96 Miles, Barry, The Beat Hotel: Ginsberg, Burroughs, and Corso in Paris, p.13
97 Family Business, p.73
98 Morgan, Bill (ed), An Accidental Autobiography: The Selected Letters of Gregory Corso, p.56
99 Family Business, p.74
100 Family Business, p.72
101 Family Business, p.71
102 Jack Kerouac and Allen Ginsberg: The Letters, p.155
103 Qtd in I Celebrate Myself, p.256
104 I Celebrate Myself, p.262
105 Family Business, p.74
106 Ginsberg, Allen, Selected Poems 1947-1995, p.72
107 The Letters of Allen Ginsberg, p.192
108 Family Business, p.77
109 I Celebrate Myself, p.262
110 Qtd in Ginsberg: A Biography, p.237
111 Family Business, p.86
112 Family Business, p.110
113 The Letters of Allen Ginsberg, p.192
114 Jack Kerouac and Allen Ginsberg: The Letters, p.393
115 The Letters of Allen Ginsberg, p.183
116 The Letters of Allen Ginsberg, p.197
117 The Letters of Allen Ginsberg, p.201
118 Letters of Allen Ginsberg and Gary Snyder, p.24
119 Family Business, p.87
120 The Letters of Allen Ginsberg, p.218
121 Family Business, p.122
122 Journals: Early Fifties Early Sixties 109
123 Jack Kerouac and Allen Ginsberg: The Letters, p.435
124 The Letters of Allen Ginsberg, p.226
125 ibid
126 The Letters of Allen Ginsberg, p.227

127 ibid
128 Family Business, p.130
129 Qtd in I Celebrate Myself, p.311
130 I Greet you at the Beginning of a Great Career, p.99
131 Wait Til I'm Dead, ebook – no page number
132 Yagé Letters, Kindle edition – no page number
133 Yagé Letters, Kindle edition – no page number
134 Yagé Letters, Kindle edition – no page number
135 Qtd in Ginsberg: A Biography, p.266
136 Qtd in Ginsberg: A Biography p.267
137 The Letters of Allen Ginsberg, p.230
138 Qtd in Ginsberg: A Biography, p.268
139 Essential Ginsberg, p.240
140 Yagé Letters, Kindle edition
141 Yage Letters, Kindle edition
142 Family Business, p.137
143 The Letters of Allen Ginsberg, p.233
144 The Letters of Allen Ginsberg, p.229

Notes on Part 3

1 Journals: Early Fifties Early Sixties, p.138–139
2 Journals: Early Fifties Early Sixties, p.186
3 Essential Ginsberg, p.356
4 I Celebrate Myself, p.328
5 Essential Ginsberg, p.358
6 Journals Early Fifties Early Sixties, p.206
7 Journals Early Fifties Early Sixties, p.207
8 Qtd in Ginsberg: A Biography p.292
9 Family Business, p.151
10 Family Business, p.160
11 The Letters of Allen Ginsberg, p.247
12 Journals Early Fifties Early Sixties,p.214
13 Journals Early Fifties Early Sixties,p.220
14 ibid
15 Qtd in Ginsberg: A Biography, p.292
16 Journals Early Fifties Early Sixties, p.230
17 Journals Early Fifties Early Sixties, p.234

18 GSL. P.40

19 I Greet You... p.127

20 Essential Ginsberg

21 Journals Early Fifties Early Sixties, p.255

22 Family Business, p.162

23 Family Business, p.165

24 Letters of Allen Ginsberg and Gary Snyder, p.42

25 Family Business, p.167

26 Qtd in Ginsberg: A Biography, p.294

27 Journals Early Fifties Early Sixties, p.261

28 Journals Early Fifties Early Sixties, p.273

29 Family Business, p.174

30 Family Business, p.174

31 ibid

32 Qtd in Trigilio, Tony, Allen Ginsberg's Buddhist Poetics, p.212

33 Ginsberg, Allen, Indian Journals, p.5

34 Essential Ginsberg, p.364

35 Qtd in Morgan, Bill, Beats Abroad, p.181

36 Family Business, p.177

37 Qtd in Ginsberg: A Biography, p.299

38 Qtd in Ginsberg: A Biography, p.297

39 Kipling, Rudyard, Kim, Kindle edition

40 Qtd in Ginsberg: A Biography, p.297

41 Qtd in Ginsberg: A Biography, p.298

42 Journals Early Fifties Early Sixties, p.266

43 Essential Ginsberg, p.289

44 Qtd In Ginsberg: A Biography, p.300

45 Indian Journals, p.10

46 Qtd in Ginsberg: A Biography, p.301

47 The Letters of Allen Ginsberg, p.260

48 Qtd in Ginsberg: A Biography, p.303

49 Qtd in Ginsberg: A Biography, p.305

50 Indian Journals, p.44

51 Family Business, p.213

52 ibid

53 Family Business, p.192

54 The Letters of Allen Ginsberg, p.274
55 The Letters of Allen Ginsberg, p.259
56 The Letters of Allen Ginsberg, p.269
57 Indian Journals, p.25
58 Indian Journals, p.38
59 Indian Journals, p.39
60 Indian Journals, p.41
61 I Greet You at the Start, p.148
62 Family Business, p.186
63 Family Business, p.185
64 I Greet You at the Start, p.148
65 Indian Journals, p.141
66 Qtd in Ginsberg: A Biography, p.309
67 Family Business, p.197
68 Qtd in Ginsberg: A Biography, p.312
69 Indian Journals, p.210
70 The Letters of Allen Ginsberg, p.259
71 Beats Abroad, p.177
72 Family Business, p.206
73 Qtd in Ginsberg: A Biography, p.318
74 Selected Letters of Allen Ginsberg and Gary Snyder, p.66
75 Qtd in Ginsberg: A Biography, p.318
76 ibid
77 In 9th June, 1963 issue
78 Family Business, p.214
79 I Celebrate Myself, p.374
80 Buddhist Poetics, p.33
81 Family Business, p.161
82 Qtd in Ginsberg: A Biography, p.320
83 Jack Kerouac and Allen Ginsberg: The Letters, p.10
84 Family Business, p.215
85 Selected Letters of Allen Ginsberg and Gary Snyder, p.70

Notes on Part 4

1 Jack Kerouac and Allen Ginsberg: The Letters, p.474
2 Selected Letters of Allen Ginsberg and Gary Snyder, p68
3 ibid

4 Jack Kerouac and Allen Ginsberg: The Letters, p.475
5 The Letters of Allen Ginsberg, p.298
6 Selected Letters of Allen Ginsberg and Gary Snyder, p.75
7 Michael Schumacher (ed.), Iron Curtain Journals: January
– May 1965, p.9
8 Family Business, p.225
9 Iron Curtain Journals, p.30
10 Family Business, p.226
11 Iron Curtain Journals, p.135
12 Iron Curtain Journals, p.108
13 Iron Curtain Journals, p.111
14 Iron Curtain Journals, p.121
15 Iron Curtain Journals, p.129
16 Family Business, p.227
17 The Letters of Allen Ginsberg, p.301
18 I Celebrate Myself, p.402
19 Family Business, p.228
20 The Letters of Allen Ginsberg, p.302
21 Family Business, p.228
22 Family Business, p.230
23 Iron Curtain Journals, p.171
24 Family Business, p.232
25 Iron Curtain Journals, p.186
26 Iron Curtain Journals, p.190
27 Iron Curtain Journals, p.192
28 Iron Curtain Journals, p.187
29 Iron Curtain Journals, p.194
30 Iron Curtain Journals, p.199
31 Iron Curtain Journals, p.216
32 Iron Curtain Journals, p.226
33 Iron Curtain Journals, p.294
34 The Letters of Allen Ginsberg, p.303
35 Iron Curtain Journals, p.284-5
36 Iron Curtain Journals, p.273
37 The Letters of Allen Ginsberg, p.304
38 The Letters of Allen Ginsberg, p.306
39 The Letters of Allen Ginsberg, p.307

40 Collected Poems, p.361
41 Miles, Barry, In the Sixties, p.71
42 The Letters of Allen Ginsberg, p.308
43 F.B.I. file - https://vault.fbi.gov/irwin-allen-ginsberg
44 http://allenginsberg.org/2015/06/allen-ginsberg-on-the-conan-obrien-tv-show/
45 Essential Ginsberg, p.274
46 Collected Poems, p.414
47 Collected Poems, p.415
48 http://ginsbergblog.blogspot.hk/2015/01/medita-tion-and-poetics-37-wales.html
49 http://ginsbergblog.blogspot.hk/2015/01/medita-tion-and-poetics-37-wales.html
50 Essential Ginsberg, p.390
51 http://ginsbergblog.blogspot.hk/2011/10/on-ezra-pounds-116th-birthday.html
52 I Celebrate Myself, p.464
53 Qtd in Ball, Gordon, East Hill Farm, p.218
54 East Hill Farm, p.54
55 Collected Poems, p.579
56 Family Business, p.319
57 Selected Letters of Allen Ginsberg and Gary Snyder, p.142
58 Selected Letters of Allen Ginsberg and Gary Snyder, p.139
59 Rosenthal, Bob, Straight Around Allen, p.26
60 Family Business, p.344
61 Selected Letters of Allen Ginsberg and Gary Snyder, p.180
62 BB book
63 Straight Around Allen, p.107
64 Selected Letters of Allen Ginsberg and Gary Snyder, p.227
65 https://www.emptymirrorbooks.com/beat/pass-ing-through-allen-ginsberg-peter-orlovsky-in-copenha-gen-january-1983
66 https://www.emptymirrorbooks.com/beat/pass-ing-through-allen-ginsberg-peter-orlovsky-in-copenha-gen-january-1983
67 I Celebrate Myself, p.577
68 ibid

69 Ginsberg, Allen, and Morgan, Bill (ed), Deliberate Prose, p.57
70 The Letters of Allen Ginsberg, p.416
71 Collected Poems, p.907
72 Collected Poems, p.937
73 The Letters of Allen Ginsberg, p.438
74 Selected Letters of Allen Ginsberg and Gary Snyder, p.307
75 Selected Letters of Allen Ginsberg and Gary Snyder, p.312-3
76 Straight Around Allen, p.144
77 Straight Around Allen, p.148
78 I Celebrate Myself, p.644
79 First Thought: Conversations with Allen Ginsberg, p.87
80 Family Business, p.308

Appendix I

List of Countries Visited by Allen Ginsberg

The following is a list of countries, and in some cases regions, visited by Allen Ginsberg, along with a date.

1. USA
2. French West Africa (present day Senegal) [1947]
3. Mexico [1951, 1953-54, 1956, 1965, 1968, 1981, 1982]
4. Cuba [1953, 1965]
5. Canada [1956, 1963, 1965, 1967, 1969, 1973, 1980, 1992]
6. Morocco [1957, 1961, 1992]
7. Spain [1957, 1992]
8. France [1957-58, 1961, 1965, 1967, 1976, 1979, 1982, 1990]
9. Italy [1957, 1967, 1979, 1981, 1982, 1990]
10. Vatican City [1957, 1967]
11. Austria [1957, 1992]
12. Germany [1957, 1976, 1978, 1979, 1982, 1983, 1992]

13. Holland [1957, 1973, 1979, 1982, 1983, 1984]
14. England [1958, 1965, 1967, 1973, 1979, 1982,
     1985, 1990, 1992]
15. Chile [1960]
16. Argentina [1960]
17. Bolivia [1960]
18. Peru [1960]
19. Panama [1960]
20. Greece [1961, 1992]
21. Israel [1961, 1988]
22. Ethiopia [1962]
23. French Somaliland (now Djibouti) [1962]
24. Tanzania [1962]
25. Kenya [1962]
26. Pakistan [1962]
27. India [1962–63, 1971]
28. Sikkim (now an Indian state) [1962]
29. Thailand [1963]
30. Vietnam [1963]
31. Cambodia [1963]
32. Hong Kong [1963]
33. Japan [1963, 1988]
34. Czechoslovakia [1965]
35. Soviet Union (present day Russia) [1965, 1985]
36. Poland [1965, 1986, 1992]
37. Wales [1967]
38. Haiti [1970]
39. Antigua [1970]
40. Bermuda [1970]
41. Virgin Islands [1970]
42. Puerto Rico [1971]

43. Fiji [1972]
44. Australia [1972]
45. Scotland [1973]
46. Belgium [1976, 1979, 1982, 1984]
47. Macedonia [1980, 1986]
48. Croatia [1980, 1986]
49. Serbia [1980, 1986]
50. Hungary [1980, 1986, 1992]
51. Switzerland [1980]
52. Nicaragua [1982, 1986]
53. Denmark [1983]
54. Sweden [1983]
55. Finland [1983]
56. Norway [1983, 1992]
57. China [1984]
58. Georgia [1985]
59. Lithuania [1985]
60. Belarus [1985]
61. Palestine [1988]
62. Turkey [1990]
63. South Korea [1990]
64. Rep. of Ireland [1992]
65. Northern Ireland [1992]
66. Czech Rep (new country) [1990, 1992]

Appendix II

The Mystery of Allen's Ginsberg's "Reading Bai Juyi"

On December 5th, 1984, while laid up sick in Shanghai, Allen Ginsberg wrote one of his lesser-known masterpieces, "Reading Bai Juyi." The poem begins by talking about Allen's first month in China, where he had been teaching and travelling after a short visit with a delegation of American writers, and ends with a short biographical piece that copies a poem by Tang Dynasty poet, Bai Juyi.

China had fascinated Ginsberg since childhood, with his interest growing in the early 1950s when he discovered the beauty of Chinese paintings and began to think of the wandering, romantic, alcoholic poets of ancient China as akin to his own Beat contemporaries. Yet despite travelling much of the globe in the following three decades, it wasn't until 1984 that he actually managed to visit China. Although beset by health problems, which were exacerbated by the horrible pollution, he managed to travel around many of the historical sites of interest from Beijing to Shanghai, Suzhou to Wuhan, and even westward to the vast provinces and Yunnan and Sichuan.

But it was in Shanghai that he wrote his great China poem. "Reading Bai Juyi" tells us about his experiences in the coal smog-covered country as he attempts to meet the locals and talk politics, all the while aware that he could never say too much, lest he end up in trouble as he had in Cuba and Czechoslovakia. He had been aware of Chinese politics since reading the *New York Times* as a young boy, and his political interest had been shaped by William S. Burroughs' introduction of Oswald Spengler's works, as well as Allen's experiences in India in the mid-sixties, where he met China's Public Enemy Number One: The Dalai Lama. Although he had at times sympathized with Mao Zedong, by the time he wrote "Reading Bai Juyi," he had come to a better understanding of the corrupt, vicious communist regime.

Ginsberg's poems from China interested me because I have been living here on-and-off since 2010. His descriptions of naïve young men and women, government brainwashing, religious oppression, and vast grey landscapes under heavy smog still ring very true today. However, it is the final section of "Reading Bai Juyi," titled "Transformation of Bai's 'A Night in Xingyang,'" that piqued my interest. While working on this book, I began looking into his time in China. I knew little about Bai Juyi and began to research his work, as it seemed clear he was important to Allen. Yet I could not find any reference online to "A Night in Xingyang."

As Ginsberg could not speak or read Chinese, he obviously read the poem in English translation. A glance at various collections of Bai and other ancient Chinese poets turned up nothing, and Google showed that the only existing reference to the poem was in books by or about Ginsberg. I began looking for alternate spellings, for during my research I found that he was terrible at getting local place names correct – and scholars usually just copy what he wrote, perpetuating these ridiculous mistakes. But I could find no close approximations. In an audio recording, I heard him pronounce it, "Xinjiang," which is the name of China's huge western province, but that didn't logically make sense. Bai was well-travelled but hadn't made the enormous trek out to the deserts of the west.

I enlisted my girlfriend to look for clues in the Chinese literature. We soon found that Bai was born and raised in a place called Xinzheng, which is close to Allen's pronunciation, if very much off from his spelling. Yet we could not find a poem under either name. Oddly, many Chinese had left comments on message boards seeking the poem, yet no one knew whether or not it existed. We thought we had a breakthrough when we uncovered various other names for the town, including "Yingyang," but still there were no poems titled "A Night in Xinzheng/Yingyang." In fact, there was a tendency among Chinese poets of the period to not title their works at all, and many modern translations are given titles by their translator.

We were working from Ginsberg's poem, which restates Bai's with Ginsberg's own biography in place of the Chinese poet, as well as comments from a reading he gave in 1994, and tried looking for poems that matched his description of the original. According to Allen, Bai grew up in the confusingly named town, then moved away as a child, only to return for one night many years later after working as a governor. We directed our research on this basis and found the real story: Bai had indeed stopped over on a trip from Suzhou to Luoyang.

Finally, we found the poem and attempted an English translation from the Chinese. Chinese characters are complex and there are numerous possible pronunciations of the first character in the place name. For our translation, we have chosen Allen's spelling of the town:

Staying the Night in Xingyang

I grew up at Xingyang and left the country paths
at a young age.
Long and far, forty years have passed;
Now again, I'm back in Xingyang for the night.
I was eleven or twelve when I left; now I'm
fifty-six.
Looking back to those childhood games,
They still flash before my eyes clearly.
The old residency has lost its place;
In the village, all of my people are gone.
Is it only the market and streets which have

changed,
Or have the hills and valleys also?
Only the green waters of Qin and You remain;
Passionless they still flow forward.

Shortly after this discovery, I also managed to track down two English translations Ginsberg may well have come across, both by Arthur Waley, who was one of the greatest translators of Chinese poetry into English. The first poem is titled "Stopping the Night at Rong-yang" and the second, "Stopping the Night at Jung-yang." No wonder it had proved so difficult to find the poem!

So where did Allen get the name, Xingyang? It could have been an interpretation by a Chinese friend or student, or perhaps even his friend, Gary Snyder, who had been on the writer's delegation at the beginning of the trip, and had helped Allen with translation. Perhaps there is another collection out there that transliterates the character as "xing." It is certainly unlikely that he ever came upon a poem with the actual title he used, but what is fascinating is that while searching Chinese message boards, there are many people even today looking for a poem titled, "A Night in Xingyang." Had they all misremembered the poem's real name, or had they read Ginsberg's poem and been sent down the same rabbit hole I had?

Translation by David S. Wills and Zhang Dandan.

Made in the USA
Middletown, DE
08 April 2021